SIMPLE STARTS

Making the Move to a
READER-CENTERED CLASSROOM

Kari Yates

HEINEMANN
Portsmouth, NH

Heinemann
361 Hanover Street
Portsmouth, NH 03801–3912
www.heinemann.com

Offices and agents throughout the world

Cataloging-in-Publication Data is on file at the Library of Congress.
ISBN: 978-0-325-06155-9

Editor: Zoë Ryder White
Development editor: Alan Huisman
Production: Hilary Goff
Cover and interior designs: Monica Ann Crigler
Cover image: Getty Images / Damir Cudic
Typesetter: Gina Poirier, Gina Poirier Design
Manufacturing: Steve Bernier

Printed in the United States of America on acid-free paper
19 18 17 16 15 EBM 1 2 3 4 5

To Kathy Cavanagh

1960–2014

*Your life's work continues
through all of us whom
you've coached and inspired.*

CONTENTS

ONLINE RESOURCES: Appendices A–E

📑 To access these printable resources, please visit
www.heinemann.com/products/E06155.aspx

Appendix A: Resources to Help You Grow Your Library

Book Ideas That Don't Cost a Dime
Sample Parent Letter to Support a Book Hunt
Book Ideas That Cost Next to Nothing
Book Ideas That Help You Get the Biggest Bang for Your Buck
Taking Stock of the Classroom Library
Reflection on Building a Better Book Collection

Appendix B: Resources to Help You Create Spaces Where Readers Will Thrive

Checklist for Creating Flexible Workspaces
Checklist for Creating a Quality Classroom Gathering Space
Anchor Chart Reflection Tool
Possible Reading Spots

Appendix C: Resources to Help You Provide Responsive Whole-Group, Small-Group, and Individual Instruction

Minilesson Planning Template
Potential Topics for Whole-Group and Small-Group Strategy Lessons
Conferring Questions to Get You Started
Weekly Conference Planning Sheet
Conference Record Sheet

Appendix D: Resources to Help You Get Kids Writing and Talking About Reading

Calendar Reading Log for K–1
My "Best Book" Log for K–1
Basic Log for Grades 1–2
Basic Log for Grades 2–5
Two-Log System for Grades 3–5
Genre Chart
Possible Future Reads
Reading Interests
Response Prompts for Writing and Talking About Reading

Appendix E: Resources to Help You Assess Your Readers from Day to Day

Two-Column Chart for Observation
Status of the Class
Roster Checklist

Acknowledgments

Near the end of this project and near the point of exhaustion, I was driving to work with the radio cranked and on came the Bill Withers hit "Lean on Me." As I started to sing along, I was overwhelmed by emotion and the realization of how many people I had leaned on, both during the eight-month sprint to put this book together and throughout my career and lifetime in ways that made this possible.

First, I must start with the children in every school I have ever had the good fortune to teach in, work in, or visit. It is seeing your joy and laughter, your triumphs, your struggles, and your simple acts of daily bravery that makes this work so absolutely urgent and rewarding. And to every teacher who ever opened his or her classroom door and let me step inside, I thank you. Oh, the magic of interacting with readers and writers in action. I've learned so much from so many.

Next, I must thank my dream-big-and-believe-in-yourself cousin, Rikka Brandon. Without her inspiration this book would not exist. Knowing both my passion for literacy and my love of writing, Rikka challenged me to find both my voice and my message by coaching me through the process of creating a book proposal.

That proposal led me to Zoë Ryder-White, talented acquisitions editor at Heinemann. Zoë's gentle guidance and fierce belief in this project nurtured the writer in me in all of the right ways. Her incredible expertise, in both content and process, made it easier to produce, rethink, deepen, expand, trim, and hang in there—and to learn all the while.

Having always loved and depended on Heinemann professional books, I now know their secret to greatness—great people. To Alan Huisman, slim and trim extraordinaire; Anthony Marvullo, editorial coordinator; Sarah Fournier, associate managing editor; Sherry Day, producer; Brett Whitmarsh, social media guru; Eric Chalek, marketing whiz; Hilary Goff, production editor; Beth Tripp, copy editor, and Monica Crigler, designer: I thank you from the bottom of my heart for treating this project with care, respect, and enthusiasm. I am so honored to become part of the amazing Heinemann family.

This book exists only because I have stood on the shoulders of my most respected mentors in the field, without ever having had the opportunity to meet any of them: Lucy Calkins, Richard Allington, Jennifer Serravallo, Kathy Collins, Debbie Miller, and Donalyn Miller. Thanks to each of you for your incredible, good-for-kids contributions to the field. I dream that someday I can shake your hand and thank you in person.

I am profoundly grateful to a core of educational leaders in my professional network whose dedication to building the best schools imaginable for kids has continually inspired me to stretch and grow: Caryl Gordy, Sarah Suchy, Julie Vomacka, Tamara Uselman, Crystal Thorson, Anne Moyano, Diana Johnson, Missy Eidsness, Jill Skarvold, Becky Sutton. Each and every one of you is a warrior for the kind of education that our children deserve. I am humbled to have been able to spend time in your presence, being mentored by your smart thinking and courageous acts on behalf of children.

About the same time I began working on the proposal for this book, my beloved friend and colleague Kathy Cavanagh launched a fiercely heroic battle with cancer. While I wrote, she fought, with both grace and grit. And although I won't be able to place a hard copy of this book in Kathy's hands, her final acts of courage gave me a new definition of bravery that I shall carry with me for a lifetime. My heart aches with missing you, Kathy. This book is dedicated to extending the work you pursued so passionately as teacher and literacy coach.

To the rest of the dear people of Heart of the Lakes Elementary School, where my love and understanding of reading workshop grew by leaps and bounds, I extend a giant hug of gratitude. You made it possible for me to experience reading workshop from many angles and perspectives. Thanks for making me a learning partner on one leg of your amazing journey. Your children are truly blessed.

I will forever owe a debt of gratitude to the staff, students, and administration of the Moorhead Area Public Schools. Our time together, both the first go-round and again now, has been a continual learning journey for me. The opportunities I was provided as a teacher in the district catapulted my passion and convictions for literacy education. A special thank-you is owed to Karla Brewster, whose guidance as my Reading Recovery teacher trainer in the late 1990s did more to shift my understanding of reading process than any other single experience.

Additional thanks are owed to Maggie Thoreson, Kristi Rowekamp, Char Lien, Kristi Ammerman, Chuck Fisher, and Amy Zanotti; the courageous and committed instructional coaches who continually help me to strengthen and clarify both my thinking and my resolve in this messy work of literacy education.

A huge thank-you to those who took time out of their own busy lives to support this project by providing work samples and photos or helping to obtain permissions: Teresa Anderson, Julie Arnold, Michelle Bormann, Kersten Buskirk, Tina Christenson, Megan Dahl, Danya Dahlin, Kim Flatau, Joan Fudge, Darla Guehna, Tracy Hein, Megan Kirchenwitz, Daidre Klinnert, Ann Kostynick, Amy Peterson, and Tammy Richter. To parents and students who gave permission to share the beautiful photos and work samples, I thank you all, and I regret that because of the trimming process many of the items do not appear in the final publication.

For anyone who has challenged my thinking through the years, whether my feathers were visibly ruffled at the time or not, I thank you. I've come to believe that each time our ideals or convictions are challenged, we somehow grow, either by making room for new ideas or by strengthening those we've committed to. For those of you who have helped me more deeply examine, reconsider, or stretch my ideas about this important work, I thank you.

If I hadn't become an independent reader myself, none of this would have been possible. And it was my sixth-grade teacher, Erin Mowers, who helped me finally find my own way to books. Thanks, Mrs. Mowers. I fell forever in love with you the day you let yourself cry while reading aloud to us. Forty years later, I still remember the feeling of community you created in our classroom through both books and kindness.

At home, I am blessed to be part of a circle of friends and family that support and sustain me in all of my endeavors.

Annika, Boden, Caden, and Zach, you bring this grandmother joy beyond measure. I rejoice in the readers you have become, but more importantly in the people you are becoming. Thanks for making the world a better place by being in it.

I thank you, Mom, for teaching me to value hard work, persistence, and the importance of giving back with a generous heart. This book is an attempt to give back to a profession I am so proud to be a part of.

I thank you, Dad, for teaching me to take risks and to keep hope alive. This entire project is dedicated to spreading hope and helping others find the courage to take the right risks.

My brother, Dean Knudson, has been the most voracious reader I've known for as far back as I can remember. Thanks, Dean, for being an astounding example of a life made richer through the power of reading.

My life has been blessed with three incredible aunts, Margaret, Kris, and Vicki, who have each in her own amazing way shaped my way of being in this world. Thanks for sharing your gifts of confidence, self-care, and affirmation.

Bushels of gratitude go out to Kathy Fisher, my "bestest bud" for a lifetime. Thanks for your unending willingness to listen to my words yet hear my unspoken message, make me laugh, let me cry, build me up, and forever see the good in what I do. You've been sitting on my shoulder the whole while, whispering in my ear, "You can do this, little buddy. I know you can."

To my amazing daughters, Erika and Briana, whose love and enduring support mean everything to me. From the time you were little you've patiently watched me walk a tightrope of balance between family and career. I am proud of this work, but it is a raindrop in the ocean compared with the love and pride I feel for each of you. Thanks for giving my life its most profound sense of purpose: raising strong daughters.

Lastly, there is John. My husband. My friend. My encourager. My biggest fan. Without you, I could not have written this book. Not just because you cooked absolutely all the meals, washed all the dishes, did all the laundry, ran all the errands, and kept me supplied with all that I needed to keep going. Not just because you helped me with those dreadful art charts and permission logs. But because your belief in me never wavered even when my own belief in myself did. I hear you playing the ukulele in the other room now and my heart swells with gratitude. How blessed I am to be so loved and cared for.

Introduction

Let's do this. It's simple to start.

> A journey of a thousand miles begins with a single step.
>
> —Laozi, Chinese philosopher

The short list of essentials for amazing reading instruction includes

* great books
* time to read and talk about them
* freedom to make choices (and mistakes) as readers
* a teacher who is willing to keep asking, "What next?"

Since you picked up this book, I'm guessing that you're already asking, "What next?"

What's next is simple.

You start to make room for more authentic reading.

You don't have to know everything about books, or reading, or even your kids.

You just need to be brave and follow a few simple steps.

You can learn more as you go.

So, come on in.

Your kids are counting on you.

It's time to bravely begin.

Oh, and by the way, it's even more fun if you find a trusted friend to take with you on the journey.

ONE

Make Room for Reading!

Simple Starting Points to Get You Going

> Of all the goals for literacy instruction, there is none more critical than creating students who read independently.
>
> —Barbara Moss and Terrell Young, *Creating Lifelong Readers Through Independent Reading*

Gear up for success with two simple (but essential) starting points for independent reading in your classroom:

1. Nurture the love of books and reading (pages 1–5).
2. Find and fiercely protect scheduled time for daily independent reading (pages 5–8).

You can do this! You can help kids fall in love with reading. You can fill your classroom with piles of amazing books kids will be itching to get their hands on. You can find stretches of time every single day during which kids will read books they care about. You can observe, respond, and interact with your readers in powerful and meaningful ways. You can make it happen, starting today.

1.1 Nurture the Love of Books and Reading

Instilling a genuine love of reading may be the most important job of any reading teacher. You can build this important foundational love of reading and books by

- ✳ reading amazing books aloud every day
- ✳ surrounding kids with books they'll want to read
- ✳ letting kids see you love and depend on books during every part of the day.

1

Read Amazing Books Aloud Every Day

Without seeing a snowboarder in action on the slopes, a child is unlikely to decide he'd like to become a snowboarder. Without hearing an accomplished violinist perform, a child has little reason to aspire to play the violin. Without regular opportunities to hear accomplished readers bring great books alive, a child won't experience the wonders reading offers.

Then Read Aloud

If you want kids to *want* to read,
Then read aloud to them.
If you want kids to fall crazy in love with great books,
Then read great books aloud to them.
If you want kids to view books as a way to learn about themselves,
Then read aloud books that mirror the soul.
If you want kids to travel to new corners of their minds,
Then read aloud stories of adventure and exploration.
If you want kids to become civil and graceful human beings,
Then read aloud tales that teach respect and human kindness.
If you want kids never to stop growing as readers,
Then never stop reading aloud.

Some lucky kids come to us with the love of reading already in bloom. They're ready to go. They've been raised on a steady diet of great books, at home and in school. These kids need teachers who will expand and nourish their growing appetites, to keep their love of books and reading alive and well.

Other kids have not been as lucky. Their experiences with books are much more limited, even negative. Some already think reading is not for them because they've experienced more struggle than success. For these kids, establishing a love of books is an absolutely crucial component to getting them back on track for success.

For kids in both of these categories, and every kid in between, the read-aloud is your most valuable tool as a reading teacher.

* It's an advertisement for becoming a real reader. It says, "Hey, look at this great thing you can do when you become a reader. This is the thing that makes all that hard work worth it!"
* It strengthens both a child's vocabulary and her or his background knowledge.
* It's an incredible way to build relationships in a community of learners.
* It exposes kids to a rich variety of genres, writing styles, authors, and topics.
* It gives children the chance to observe a skilled reader negotiating the strategies and techniques of making meaning from print.
* It exposes kids to the hidden world inside a reader's head as the reader thinks aloud.

✻ It gives everyone in the room a rich, common experience. Even the most struggling readers come along risk free, accessing more complex texts than they are yet able to tackle on their own.

✻ It primes the pump for independence.

A kindergarten teacher wonders: "My kids can't sit still long enough for a twenty-minute read-aloud. I have to choose very short, simple texts, and even then they get restless."

A possible solution: Ask your colleagues to help you find books your kids will sit still for. The media specialist or the teacher next door can be a great resource. Quality matters much more than length. Then, once you find great books, make every read-aloud a great performance. Put your all into reading with dramatic expression, using varied volume, pitch, and intonation. If kids can't sit still till the end of a longer book, look for a great stopping point and end with "to be continued." The anticipation will bring them back the next day ready and eager to tune in for more.

A fifth-grade teacher wonders: "Reading chapter books aloud is a huge time commitment, and my kids have outgrown picture books."

A possible solution: Chapter books are the mainstay of intermediate-grade teachers' read-alouds, but kids are never too old for well-written picture books. Picture books offer amazingly rich literary language structures and vocabulary. They can be used to teach all the same literary structures of longer books but in less time. Ask your librarian for suggestions. Eventually, you'll probably want to mix in some longer works, but never apologize for sharing picture books with older students.

Including poetry as a read-aloud is another way to balance longer works.

In *Igniting a Passion for Reading*, Steven L. Layne suggests that the read-aloud is one of the best ways to lure readers into loving books:

> In terms of our disengaged readers, those who can read but don't,
> being read to is one of the most seductive . . . methods of bringing
> them to books. To reach these kids, we're going to have to impact the

way they think about books and the way they feel about books. . . .
We need to put them in a situation where being with books is
pleasurable. What could be more pleasurable than a great book read
aloud by a passionate reader? (2009, 53)

Making the following promises to yourself and your students will do more to advance the
love of reading than almost any other actions you could take.

The Read-Aloud Promises

I promise to read aloud to my students every day we are together.

I promise to choose amazing books.

I promise to gather my kids around me as a community of learners.

I promise to pace the reading, taking time for conversation along the way.

I promise to make my reading engaging.

I promise to think aloud as I read aloud.

I promise to share the feelings the text makes me feel.

I promise to let kids relax and enjoy the experience for what it is.

I promise to arrange for and insist that every child be included.

I promise to begin today.

Surround Kids with Books They'll Want to Read

To teach reading, you need books—great books. No matter what other programs or materials you use in your reading instruction, you're going to need stacks and piles and baskets
and bushels of books. Your classroom book collection is the equivalent of a chef's pantry.
Funnel every resource you can into stocking your classroom pantry with loads of great books.
Depending on the school library or the guided reading book collection is not enough. *Every*
classroom needs an amazing collection of books in a variety of genres, topics, shapes, sizes,
and readability levels.

Later in the book I address the absolute importance of choice. But before choice can matter,
you need to start stocking your shelves. If your current collection is meager and bedraggled, you
may think that bushels and baskets of great books are unattainable, especially since you probably have a measly budget as well. But don't despair. This is doable, and you can get there faster
than you think. See Appendix A, "Resources to Help You Grow Your Library" (available online at
www.heinemann.com/products/E06155.aspx), for dozens of ways to accumulate books for your
classroom collection, organized into three categories:

* ideas that don't cost a dime
* ideas that cost next to nothing
* ideas to help you get the biggest bang for your buck.

Let Kids See You Love and Depend on Books Throughout Every Part of the Day

Students need to see you depend on books as much as you depend on pencils or paper. Following is a sampling of things you can let your students see you do with books to make sure they get a strong and consistent message about the value of books in your life.

Things Kids Need to See You Do with Books

Read aloud every single day of the year, at least once, no matter what.

Use books to create a sense of family and community in the classroom.

Demonstrate reverence in the handling and care of books.

Use books purposefully to teach about a topic.

Hunt for needed information in books.

Share books that amuse and entertain you.

Laugh until you cry because of a book.

Hurt until you cry because of a book.

Inhale the smell of a brand-new book and marvel over the beauty of it.

Hug and protect a beloved old book, ragged as it may be.

Shake with the excitement of wanting to tell about what you've read.

Celebrate the arrival of new additions to the classroom collection.

Use one book to launch another.

Connect with other people through books.

STARTING POINT 1.2 Find and Fiercely Protect Scheduled Time for Daily Independent Reading

To become strong independent readers, students need to spend big chunks of uninterrupted time reading independently *every single day*. For that to happen, you need to get independent reading on the schedule; keep it there; and honor it every day as sacred.

Kids Learn to Read by Reading

We learn to play basketball by spending time on the court. We learn to swim by spending time in the water. And we learn to read by holding books in our hands and spending time with our eyes on print.

After all, isn't helping students become independent lifelong readers what reading instruction is really about? That's the big goal, right? Everything else you do in the reading classroom is simply there to support successful independent reading in college, career, and life.

The More Kids Read, the Better They Become at Reading

"It is worth emphasizing that the most important single activity to promote reading *is reading*. Several studies have shown that having students read an additional 280,000 words per year can mean the difference between scoring at the 20th percentile and scoring at the 50th" (Schmoker 2001). Numerous research studies have proven that time spent reading improves students' comprehension skills, background knowledge, vocabulary, fluency, and writing ability (Krashen 2004). The formula is simple: the more time students spend with "eyes on text," the better readers they become (Stahl 2004, 190). And it's not just a matter of ability; the act of reading contributes to cognitive growth (Cunningham and Stanovich 2001).

Imagine independent reading as the sun, the center of the reading solar system, and all the other parts of reading instruction as planets revolving around it. Every single thing you do in the reading classroom should be aimed at improving your students' ability to read independently. On the flip side, everything you observe and learn about your students during independent reading should guide and inform the other reading instruction you provide.

For example, phonics and word study are essential, but not on their own. They matter because they help students successfully comprehend while reading independently. Strategy instruction and fluency matter *only* because they enable the child to succeed as a real reader. Independent reading cannot be pushed to the borders of the classroom while "other stuff" takes precedence. It needs to be the central focus of your reading instruction. (See Figure 1.1.)

Figure 1.1 Independent Reading as the Central Focus of Reading Instruction

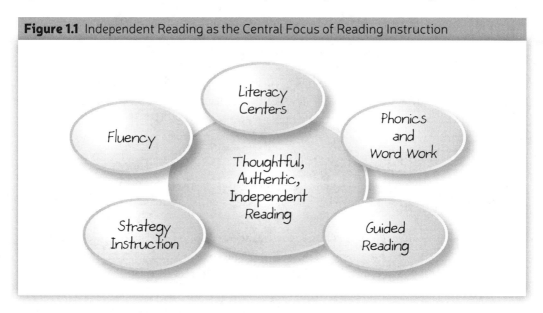

Does independent reading already have a place in your class schedule? If so, does it shine like the sun, or is it hidden in the shadows? The chart in Figure 1.2 will help you think about how much time you'll eventually want to devote to daily independent reading. It also suggests how much time to allocate for the brief teaching point, often called a minilesson, that you'll want to provide each day before independent reading begins and the brief reflection on reading, or share time, you'll include to end independent reading each day.

Figure 1.2 Target Goals for Time Spent Supporting Independent Reading

Time Goals (in Minutes)* by Grade for Independent Reading

Grade	Brief Teaching Point Before Reading		Independent Reading		Reflection After Reading	Total	
K	Fall 5	→ Spring 10	Fall 10	→ Spring 25	5	Fall 20	→ Spring 40
1	Fall 5	→ Spring 10	Fall 15	→ Spring 35	5	Fall 25	→ Spring 50
2	Fall 10	→ Spring 15	Fall 20	→ Spring 40	5	Fall 35	→ Spring 60
3–6	Fall 10	→ Spring 15	Fall 30	→ Spring 40	5	Fall 45	→ Spring 60

*Ranges indicate the progression from fall to spring.

To Find Time to Read, Something's Got to Go

With schedules that are already jam-packed, all of this is possible only by steering clear of activities that are less important and less powerful than real reading. Think about activities that often take up valuable minutes in the reading classroom: worksheets, crossword puzzles, word searches, cut-and-paste activities, coloring pages. None of these activities honors what study after study has concluded about how kids learn to read. They need books in their hands. Books they *can* and *want* to read.

As pointed out by Schmoker in his article "The Crayola Curriculum" (2001), the unfortunate reality of many literacy classrooms is that way too much other stuff is taking place in the name of literate activity. The problem is not with *how much* time we have but with *how we use* the time we have. Wishing for more time is futile. So, making different choices about how you spend the time you have is the only solution.

Kids can't learn to read at the level required for success if they are not spending the majority of the time authentically reading real texts and talking and writing about their reading. The formula for learning to read is clear:

time + good-fit books + thinking, talking, and writing = success

Not one teacher reading this book picked it up because she or he had an extra chunk of time and wondered what to do with it. Everyone who ever found more time for independent reading started off wondering where the time could possibly come from. But the good news is thousands of teachers have figured it out, and you can too. Here are five simple starting points to help you reclaim precious minutes for independent reading:

1. **Tighten up transitions.** You can "find" an extra ten to twenty minutes each day by sticking to the schedule and making clean transitions. Trim three minutes from bathroom break, another two when the kids get back from music or art, and a few more by shortening the snack break, and you've already grabbed an extra six to seven minutes.

2. **Trim some fat.** If there's no single activity you can completely eliminate, trim five or ten minutes from several. This adds up quickly.

3. **Integrate social studies and science with reading.** Supplement your science and social studies instruction by reading aloud high-quality historical fiction, biographies, and expository texts. Integrate content area learning into independent reading by stocking your classroom library shelves with nonfiction related to social studies and science.

4. **Have kids read while you are working with small groups.** You are probably already working with guided reading groups or providing other small-group instruction. So, rather than having kids engage in center work or stations during this time, gradually introduce independent reading as the *primary* activity for the rest of the class during this time.

5. **Eliminate artificial activities.** Reclaim any time spent filling out worksheets and workbooks. These are not authentic tasks. By substituting real independent reading, you'll not only help your kids grow as readers but also have a whole lot less "correcting" to do at the end of the day.

Reflect on Finding Time

* Whom can you ask to help you evaluate your current schedule?
* How much time are you able to find *today* in which your students can read independently?
* Where can you find additional "lost" minutes?
* What is most likely to interfere with your ability to protect this time once you find it?
* Which of the activities that you are considering trading or adjusting to accommodate daily independent reading is the hardest to let go of? Why?

Reflect on Chapter 1

You're ready! You're committed to finding the time to make independent reading happen consistently each day. You've committed to a daily read-aloud. You've surrounded your kids with great books and made sure your kids know how much you value and depend on these books. Books on your shelves and time on your schedule! You're ready to bravely begin an amazing journey.

But before we dig in, take a moment to do a pinky swear. Pinky swear you won't give up when this gets bumpy. Because it probably *will* get bumpy. Hang in there and move forward with courage and commitment. Before you know it, you'll have some days where *pretty good* will replace *bumpy* and then some days where *just plain amazing* will replace *pretty good*. Please just don't give up before the amazing things start to happen. Your kids are counting on you.

Now take a moment and reflect on the starting points in this chapter. (See Figure 1.3.)

Next, using the reflections in Figure 1.3, list two or three manageable actions you can commit to, *starting today*, to help you achieve these goals. Keep the time line short enough so you don't lose momentum. (See Figure 1.4.)

Figure 1.3 Chapter 1 Reflection and Goal Setting

The Goals	Reflections
Reading aloud. I have made the read-aloud promises and am committed to using this valuable tool to nurture and develop the love of books and reading.	
Collecting books. I am working to surround my kids with great books throughout the classroom and the learning day. I am committed to knowing my collection so that I can develop it in smart ways.	
Setting aside time. I have designated a chunk of time in my daily schedule (twenty to sixty minutes, depending on how old my students are) for independent reading.	

Figure 1.4 Chapter 1 Action Steps

What I Commit to Do	Helpful Resources	Realistic Time Line

TWO

CREATE SPACES THAT HELP READERS FLOURISH

> Classroom environments are organic—they grow as we do. The best of them
> reflect the hearts and souls of those who inhabit them. They're never really
> finished. They're never really "done." How could they be, when every day
> students and teachers learn something new?
>
> —Debbie Miller, *Teaching with Intention: Defining Beliefs,*
> *Aligning Practice, Taking Action, K–5*

Support independent reading by thoughtfully designing the physical environment:

1. Arrange workspaces with flexibility in mind (pages 12–15).
2. Build community by creating a classroom gathering place (pages 16–18).
3. Select and prepare an accessible and appealing physical space for your library (pages 18–19).
4. Use anchor charts to strengthen the learning (pages 19–22).

From the first moment they step into your classroom, students will be looking for visual clues about what they can expect. Is it welcoming? Warm? Comfortable? Safe? What kind of learning will take place here? Not only is the environment you create for your students an important backdrop, but in many ways it shapes the experiences that take place within it. The physical space of the classroom can be used to convey important messages. (See Figure 2.1.)

Transforming four walls, a jumble of furniture, and those stacks and piles of books you've been collecting into a space that will welcome children and nurture them as they become self-directed learners may require you to roll up your sleeves and shake things up a little. The four elements most essential to creating a physical environment in which your young readers will flourish are flexible workspaces, a gathering place, the classroom library, and anchor charts.

11

Figure 2.1 Positive Messages Conveyed Through the Environment	
The Message	**How You Might Communicate It**
This is our shared home during the school day.	Display student work and include students in decisions about space and routines.
This is a safe place.	Keep the space neat and orderly. Establish a schedule that moves smoothly from one meaningful activity to the next.
You are important. There is a special spot for you to call your own.	Designate and clearly label a spot for each child to work and safely store her or his belongings.
We will have fun here.	Smile, laugh, and show outward signs that you enjoy the time you spend with your students.
Independence is valued here. Therefore, I want you to have access to the tools you need.	Store the materials students need in places that are easy to reach.
Many times we will gather as a whole group. There is a special spot for that.	Create a welcoming gathering spot large enough for the whole class as a central feature of your classroom.
I want you to be comfortable.	Provide a number of comfortable and inviting places for students to read and work throughout the classroom.
We love books and make them the center of our learning.	Store and display books in all parts of the classroom.
By sharing our ideas and thinking together, we do our best learning.	Display anchor charts cocreated by you and your students that capture important learning.
Because we value our environment, we work together to care for it.	Establish and teach explicit expectations in which students become partners in caring for the environment.
We value interaction.	Provide a variety of spaces that support comfortable, face-to-face interaction and collaboration for partnerships and small groups.

 ## Arrange Workspaces with Flexibility in Mind

When I was in elementary school, we sat in the same desks in the same rows all day long. We saw a lot of the teacher's face but mostly stared at the backs of classmates' heads. We didn't get much chance to move or make choices, and opportunities to interact with peers were almost nonexistent. To connect directly with a classmate during class, we had to sneak in a whisper or slip a secret note. The rows and columns of student desks suggested that learning was an isolated and fixed process rather than a collaborative and open-ended one.

I get a little bit wiggly and inattentive just thinking about it, don't you? Today we're a whole lot smarter about classroom design, learning styles, and student preferences. We know our classrooms need to be arranged in ways that make a variety of whole-class, small-group, partner, and individual work a natural and manageable part of the day. We know our kids need chances to connect and interact easily and frequently, moving about the classroom throughout the day and working in various locations.

As you arrange your classroom to accommodate interaction and instruction that best support independent reading, you'll want to create spaces in which students can work

* in teacher-facilitated small groups of two to six students
* independently in small groups and partnerships
* by themselves away from distractions.

Step Inside a Classroom

Flexible Spaces in Room 2B

When second grader Nathan enters the room in the morning, he makes his lunch selection on the interactive whiteboard and joins his tablemates at his assigned spot at the blue table. The four children have a conversation about the topic of the day, which is posted on the board. When his teacher, Mrs. Moon, has completed her morning record keeping, she calls the students to the gathering area for a read-aloud followed by a minilesson about book choice. Afterward, Nathan gets his book box and goes to a vacant beanbag chair to read independently. His classmates are scattered around the room, some at tables, some on the floor, others in soft seating. While Nathan is reading, Mrs. Moon gathers three students at an empty table and gives them additional support in how to identify books that are right for them. A group of four boys who have formed a book club sit in the gathering space, huddled around a tub of books about snakes, the club's topic. About twenty-five minutes later, Nathan joins his partner for buddy reading in their designated spot in the classroom library. Then the entire class reconvenes in the gathering area and reflects on how the reading went today.

During just over an hour, many of the same spaces in the classroom have been comfortably shared and reused by many different students for different purposes. Nathan's teacher definitely understands the importance of supporting readers through flexible spaces.

Spaces for Teacher-Facilitated Small Groups

While your students are reading independently, you will sometimes want to work with a small group (see Chapter 8). Many teachers have a special table in their classroom for small-group work, with teaching materials such as magnetic letters, dry-erase boards, and writing utensils within easy reach. Others, especially when space is at a premium, keep these materials in a wheeled cart or basket they can move to a variety of spaces. Let personal preferences and circumstances be your guides.

Spaces for Students to Work Independently in Small Groups and Partnerships

As you implement independent reading in your classroom, you'll discover more and more reasons for students to work collaboratively. Sometimes you'll encourage and facilitate student groups centered on books (book clubs, for example). Other times, partnerships and small groups will crop up spontaneously as students discover books and topics they want to explore more deeply. Debbie Miller (2008) puts it like this:

> And working independently doesn't always mean working in isolation. Having areas where children can get together to discuss big ideas, solve problems, research a topic of mutual interest, or learn to read and talk about a book together can enhance their understanding and help them construct meaning through conversation and collaboration. (33)

Spaces for Students to Work by Themselves Away from Distractions

Sharing a crowded space with dozens of other kids all day can be wearing. Sometimes kids just need to get away from it all. Every classroom needs places that provide a higher degree of privacy and concentration when students need it. These spaces don't need to be elaborate; they just require a little imagination and willingness to rethink traditional ideas about workspaces. Examples include the following:

* a small desk pushed up against a wall and enclosed by a trifold cardboard divider
* a soft chair or beanbag nestled behind a bookshelf or other natural divider
* the denlike space underneath a table pushed against a wall.

Flexible thinking is the key to flexible spaces. A few simple adjustments in the way you arrange your classroom can go a long way toward creating more student-friendly learning experiences for twenty-first-century kids. Using spaces flexibly doesn't have to be chaotic or unstructured.

Let Go of "Single-Use" Thinking

Spaces can be used in different ways at different times of day. Very few teachers have as much classroom space as they wish. But even spacious classrooms have areas that can wear different hats throughout the day:

* A table used for small-group instruction during independent reading can later be a place for students who want to spread out and work on a writing project.
* Classroom library shelves are a natural division from the distractions of the classroom and create a space in which a small group or partners can work.
* The classroom gathering area can accommodate several partnerships or two small groups when it's not being used for whole-class activities.

Consider Comfort and Interaction

When adults gather to work on a project, they want to be comfortable; have room to spread out if they need to; and be able to see, hear, and interact with everyone in the group. Kids are no different.

* Tables can be used in many different ways and lend themselves to both spreading out and collaboration.
* If you don't have tables, you can easily push desks into clusters to achieve the same effect.
* Beanbags, comfy upholstered chairs, and cushions, scattered throughout the classroom, are great spots for one or two students to read and work together.

Teach Students to Be Respectful of the Spaces They Use

For shared spaces to work, students need to be good guests when they visit someone else's table or use common classroom areas. So, you'll want to teach and reinforce your expectations:

* When sitting at someone else's desk, students should use their own or community writing utensils.
* When leaving a small-group workspace, students should double-check that they have left the space looking as good as or better than they found it.

The checklist for creating flexible workspaces in Appendix B (available online at www .heinemann.com/products/E06155.aspx) will help you reflect on the specifics of your classroom arrangement and choose some next steps.

2.2 Build Community by Creating a Classroom Gathering Place

Every classroom needs an area that allows the entire class to come together as a school family. In literacy-rich classrooms, this is where read-alouds and whole-group lessons take place, where students can share, listen, talk, and learn from one another. For teachers who value interaction and wish to create a true sense of community in their classroom, the gathering space is nonnegotiable, even if space is tight. Figure 2.2 lists some ideas to think about when planning for this area.

Appendix B (available online at www.heinemann.com/products/E06155.aspx) includes a checklist to help you design a quality gathering space. Here are some additional tips:

* **Sit in a circle whenever you can.** A circle instantly creates a community of equals in which each member can see and be seen by all the others. It takes more space than some other configurations but is definitely worth it. Of course, sometimes you'll want your students to gather in a clump so they can better see a chart, book, or other central focus of instruction.
* **Consider the age of your students.** Younger students may need assigned spots indicated by marks on the floor. Older students require more space.

Figure 2.2

Basic Considerations for the Gathering Space	
Access to teaching materials	You need easy access to chart paper, sticky notes, a document camera, whiteboards, markers, and pencils.
An easel with a shelf for supplies	An easel that provides both a sturdy surface for your chart paper and a place to keep your supplies is ideal. If you have one, lucky you! If you don't, improvise by organizing your teaching supplies in a plastic bucket and taping your chart paper to the vertical surface of your chalkboard or whiteboard.
A comfortable place to sit while you teach	Rather than stand, settle yourself in a favorite chair or on a stool. Doing so tells your students, "We are in this together. I am part of this community of learners, too."
Space for everyone	The space needs to be large enough to accommodate all your students, either in a circle or as a more closely spaced group (ideally, they should be able to do both).
Limited distractions	The space should be at a distance from obvious distractions (the classroom door, for example), and all students should easily be able to see you and any teaching material you display.
A basket of books you've already read aloud	The gathering space is a great place to keep a basket full of books you and your students have enjoyed together as a class. Students will know right where to find their favorites.

* **Use a rug or carpet remnant.** An area rug of some kind (even if your classroom has wall-to-wall carpeting) helps define the gathering space. It doesn't have to be fancy. Carpet remnants are inexpensive, and many discount stores carry large area rugs.
* **Add some charm.** Adding special touches (a plant or two, soft lighting, cushions, etc.) makes the space more inviting and comfortable. You're going to spend a lot of time together in the space, so make it special.
* **Think outside the box.** If you're having difficulty envisioning where you could create a gathering spot in your classroom, ask a colleague to help you brainstorm. Try a few options. A Google or Pinterest search for images of classroom gathering spaces will bring up hundreds of photos. Check out Figure 2.3 for one example.

Figure 2.3 Anatomy of a Classroom Gathering Space

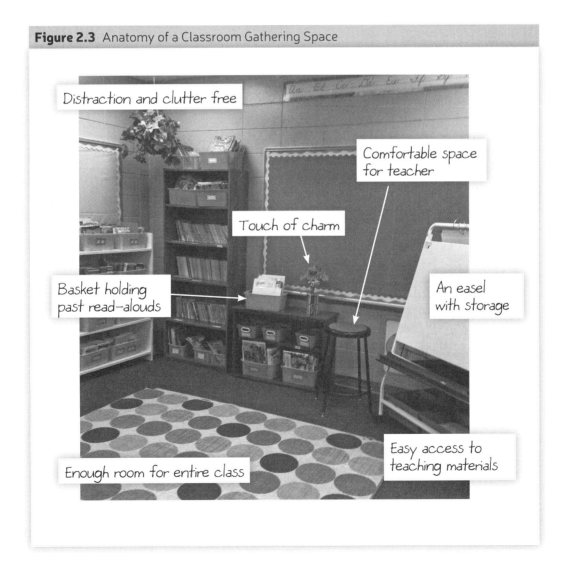

A fourth-grade teacher wonders: *"My kids are big and my classroom is small. I simply don't have the space for a gathering area in my classroom. Besides, isn't it easier for kids to focus from their desks than in a crowded clump?"*

A possible solution: The bigger the kids, the more able they are to move desks or tables to temporarily create space in which to gather as a group. Kids love this heavy work and can be taught to do it quickly and efficiently. Although it may feel simpler for students to remain in their individual desks during a read-aloud or reading lesson, gathering together more closely makes interaction, partner work, and true engagement easier and more genuine. Kids also appreciate the change of pace and a chance to move around.

STARTING POINT 2.3 Prepare an Accessible, Appealing Space for Your Library

Soon it will be time to take all the books you've been accumulating and transform them from stacks and rows and piles into something you can proudly call a classroom library.

Some libraries start out as a humble little bookcase with two or three shelves; others are built from enormous existing resources. But, no matter how humble or great your current classroom book collection is, keep the following goals in mind as you select the perfect space:

- ✳ **Give the classroom library a place of honor.** Don't relegate it to a dusty back corner or the shelves nestled behind the guided reading table. Place it center stage. These books are the heart and soul of the independent reading program in your classroom.
- ✳ **Make it easily accessible.** Locating the library in an area that is crowded or difficult to get to will limit its use. Place the books in an area that is easily approached from several directions, has room for several students to browse at one time, and allows students to squat or sit in front of the shelves without imposing on someone else's space.
- ✳ **Make it inviting.** You needn't go crazy, but consider simple ways to make your library inviting. Place it near a window. Remove any visual clutter. Define the space with a small area rug, or place beanbags or other comfortable seating nearby. Display favorite or thematic books on the tops of shelves. You want this space to have a good feel. You want kids to *want* to spend time here.

✻ **Leave room to grow.** As you get the word out that you are hungry for books and keep your eyes peeled for good deals (check out the ideas in Appendix A, available online at www.heinemann.com/products/E06155.aspx), your collection will grow at a surprising pace. Start planning for growth right away. Make sure there are simple ways to expand when you need more space. This way you'll feel joyful instead of frustrated when you face the welcome problem of finding ways to integrate all the new books that are finding their way to your classroom door.

2.4 Use Anchor Charts to Strengthen Learning

Anchor charts are simple paper charts you create with your students. They capture learning in a visible way and make it memorable in the moment and accessible in the future. Making learning visible is not a new concept. You no doubt have lots of posters and charts on the walls of your classroom already. You display visuals on chalkboards, whiteboards, projectors, and screens. So what's the big deal about anchor charts?

As primitive as they may seem in a twenty-first-century classroom, simple charts on white paper, created with colored markers and a few stick figures, have incredibly powerful advantages as teaching and learning tools:

✻ **Real-time learning.** Because you make them right before kids' eyes, your students' learning experience is directly connected with the content of the chart. Reusing or purchasing charts isn't nearly as powerful as creating a chart in real time.

✻ **Precision.** Because you can reinforce the exact language *you* use in your teaching and focus on what *you* choose as most important, you don't have to settle for "close enough" or "how I taught it last year." The visual precisely matches today's learning.

✻ **Lasting connections.** Charts don't get erased at the end of the day or the end of the period. You create them over time, adding to them from one day to the next. Students see that learning is connected from day to day.

✻ **Useful reference tools.** Posted in accessible places, your anchor charts become powerful reference tools on future days, during future lessons.

✻ **Engagement.** Anchor charts are not just visual clutter or pretty decoration. By incorporating photos, student work samples, student names, and other artifacts from your classroom, you turn them into truly meaningful and engaging tools for learning.

✻ **Uncluttered learning.** The clean language and visual elements of a chart cut through the noise, simplifying learning to its most essential elements. Although all students benefit, this is especially helpful for English language learners, students with auditory processing difficulties, and students who have a stronger visual learning style. Charts are the anchors that help kids solidify and apply learning.

The suggestions in Figure 2.4 will help you avoid making some common mistakes with charts.

Figure 2.4 Common Anchor Chart Mistakes and How to Avoid Them

Common Mistake	What to Do Instead
Creating the chart in advance	Co-construct the chart with your students. Think of an anchor chart as a way to bullet important instructional points as they're made.
Trying to save time by laminating a chart and using it over and over, from one year to the next	Give all students the chance to watch learning become visual before their eyes. For them, much of the power of charts is seeing the words and symbols go onto the paper at the moment of learning.
Thinking every chart has to be beautiful or perfect	Remember that beautiful and perfect are not as important as simple, cocreated, and meaningful.
Forgetting to give the chart a title that summarizes the big idea	Give every chart a clear, simple title that helps students remember in an instant the powerful learning it holds.
Filling all the white space on a chart with words, using long sentences and even paragraphs	Capture the learning in short sentences, summary phrases, and bullets, leaving plenty of white space. Less is more.
Using only words on a chart	Keep in mind the power of nonlinguistic representation (Marzano 2012) as an effective learning strategy. Simple drawings, stick figures, and icons help the learning stick (Martinelli and Mraz 2012).
Creating charts on a whiteboard or chalkboard and erasing them after the lesson	Create your anchor charts on chart paper. After they are complete, post them where children can refer to them as needed in the future.
Keeping too many charts up at one time, creating a visually distracting classroom	Limit the number of charts in your classroom to no more than ten at a time. If your kids still want to be able to refer to older charts, clip them onto clothes hangers and hang several on the same hook. Kids can flip through and find the one they need.

In their amazing book *Smarter Charts* (2012), Marjorie Martinelli and Kristine Mraz show teachers how to use charts to boil down "abstract content and represent it in a concrete way" by weaving a few carefully selected words together into a powerful visual representation. They suggest three types of charts to help your students become stronger independent readers:

* charts to teach routines
* charts to teach strategies
* charts to teach processes.

See Figures 2.5 through 2.7 for examples of each of these types of charts.

Figure 2.5 Anchor Chart to Teach Routine: Get Started

Figure 2.6 Anchor Chart to Teach Strategy: Making Character Inferences

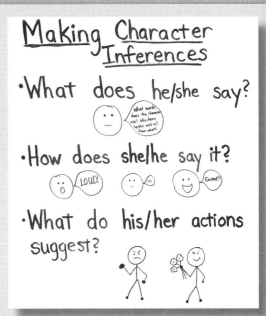

Figure 2.7 Anchor Chart to Teach Process: Partner Talk

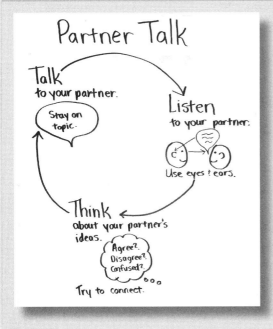

You probably won't be surprised by what I'm about to say. The only way to explore using anchor charts is to jump in and try it. Get yourself some chart paper and some nice juicy markers in colors you love and give it a whirl. Don't expect works of art. After you've tried out a couple of anchor charts, use the anchor chart reflection in Appendix B (available online at www.heinemann.com/products/E06155.aspx) to think about how it's going.

Seven Simple Steps to Get You Started with Anchor Charts

1. **Choose a teaching point.** Consider what you will teach in the coming days and select content that will be useful to anchor with a chart: A routine? A strategy? A process? The chart is a tool to facilitate the learning. The teaching comes first; the chart supports it.

2. **Select a title.** Choose a meaningful title that clearly states how the chart can help a student. Think bumper sticker: short, clear, descriptive ("Gathering-Spot Agreements," "Reading with a Partner," "Solving a Tricky Word").

3. **Build the chart *during* a lesson or series of lessons.** "I was thinking it would be good for us to make a chart to help us remember what we're learning."

4. **Use short, clean language.** Charts are a form of note taking. Less is more. Include only the essential language.

5. **Make it pop.** Use color in strategic ways. Create a visual link by using stick figures, photos, diagrams, and icons. The goal is to make the chart as visually clean and powerful as you can.

6. **Teach *how* to use the chart.** Explicitly teach how, when, and why students might use the chart. "When we turn and talk from now on, refer to this chart as a reminder of the things strong partners do."

7. **Post it.** When you post the chart, be sure to put it in a smart location—highly visible in a logical place given the topic. "I'll post this chart about book selection right in the library where you can refer to it while you're choosing books."

Reflect on Chapter 2

Classroom spaces are always works in progress. To create an environment that supports independent reading, you need to be willing to try things out and make adjustments as you see how your students respond. It takes time to figure out what works with your unique room, your furnishings, and your students. Successful teachers see their physical environment as a tool that can be constantly tweaked to accommodate the changing demands of their students, their teaching style, and their instructional goals. Keep this in mind as you create spaces that nurture independent reading, writing, thinking, and conversation. Before you move on, take time to implement some of the action steps you've identified throughout the chapter. (See Figure 2.8.)

Figure 2.8 Chapter 2 Goals, Reflections, and Next Steps

The Goals	Reflections and Next Steps
Flexible workspaces. I've created a variety of flexible workspaces to support small-group, partner, and individual learning and interaction. My students experience both choice and variety in their workspaces.	
Gathering space. I have created a gathering space that allows the entire learning community to gather comfortably. Everything I need for teaching is easily within reach.	
Classroom library space. I've selected a classroom library space that is both appealing and accessible.	
Anchor charts. I've begun to use anchor charts to strengthen and anchor important learning. I've found ways to make anchor charts available to my students for future reference.	

THREE

BRING OUT THE BEST IN YOUR READERS

Because we want our students to be readers for life and not just readers in school, our expectations must be high. They must also be clear and rigorous. After all, we're aiming to affect lives and thinking habits, not just test scores and state rankings.

—Kathy Collins, *Growing Readers: Units of Study in the Primary Classroom*

Bring out the best in your readers by focusing on two critical areas:

1. Build positive relationships with and among your students (pages 24–28).

2. Teach expectations with patience and consistency (pages 28–33).

To help children truly flourish, not just as readers, writers, mathematicians, historians, and scientists but as human beings, you must dig deep, drawing on all you know as a teacher. Shaping an eclectic roster of students into a caring community of self-directed learners takes time, love, and patience. Bringing out the best in every learner is complex and ongoing work that brings you face-to-face with the heart and soul of your beliefs and intentions as an educator.

3.1 Build Positive Relationships with and Among Your Students

Take a good look at the faces in your classroom. They aren't last year's kids. They aren't the class next door. These are your kids. They are with you for an entire year, and every day they'll be watching for signs that you are falling in love with them, both as individuals and as this year's class. They'll be looking for signs that you fiercely believe in them and see their potential great-ness. Each day they'll look to you for direction and for clues as to the sort of place this is and the sort of teacher you are. Each day they'll wonder:

* Does my teacher understand and care about me?
* Does my teacher notice what's truly special about me?
* Will I make connections with other students?
* Will I know what to do?
* Will I be successful?
* Will what I do here be interesting and fun?

When all the children in your classroom can answer a resounding yes to all the questions on this list, chances are things will run pretty smoothly. If you and your students want to become a caring and united daytime family, connecting through stories, laughter, struggles, and the joy of learning, you'll need to put relationships first.

Ideas to Strengthen Relationships in the Reading Classroom

* Greet students personally every day.
* Build trust through consistent daily actions.
* Position content under an umbrella of caring.
* Use books and conversation to strengthen the community.
* Use reading conferences to support and understand individual students.
* Fill the day with joyful interactions.

Step Inside a Classroom

Connecting with Students upon Arrival

It is 7:55 and students are busy at their lockers, peeling off layers of mittens, scarves, hats, and boots. Ms. Andres is in the hallway, cheerfully greeting students. She tells Noah how glad she is to see he remembered snow pants today; she checks in with Emma about her sick cat, with Charity about her dance recital. Will wants to tell another story about his new baby brother, and Mrs. Andres listens, patient and smiling. Sophia announces that her grandmother is coming for a visit, and Ms. Andres notices aloud that Aiden has flashy new tennis shoes. These quick greetings and conversations let Ms. Andres' students know she's glad to see them, has been thinking about them, and is interested in the things that are important to them.

Greet Students Personally Every Day

Meeting your students at the door or the lockers each morning is one of the simplest ways to build positive relationships with them. When you greet each and every student warmly and individually, calling him or her by name and connecting through conversation, you help everyone start the day feeling welcome and connected.

Build Trust Through Consistent Daily Actions

Learning to read requires tremendous amounts of courage from your students. It is a continual sequence of effort and risk. Therefore, few things matter more than your willingness to invest the time and energy needed to earn their trust. Figure 3.1 outlines some consistent teacher actions that build trust in the reading classroom.

Figure 3.1 Daily Actions to Build Trust

Consistent Teacher Actions	Examples
Follow a predictable schedule.	Post a daily schedule that children can follow and depend on. If independent reading is scheduled for 10:00, make sure it happens at 10:00. On the rare occasion that it doesn't, alert students to the change and explain why it's necessary.
Be true to your word.	If you tell a child he can show his special rock at the end of the day, follow through. If you say you're going to confer with a certain student on Tuesday, make sure he can count on having that special one-to-one time with you on Tuesday.
Respect the dignity of children.	Avoid reprimanding students in front of a group. Assume the best of your students, not the worst. Don't focus primarily on what they can't do; figure out what they can do and build from there.
Teach explicitly and release responsibility gradually (Pearson and Gallagher 1983).	Don't expect students to move abruptly from the first demonstration to being able to do something independently. Move gradually from modeling to guiding to supporting students as they try things on their own. Use a mix of whole-group, small-group, and individual instruction.
Don't ask a student to do work that isn't right for her or him.	Provide good-fit books across a range of interests, readabilities, and genres. Don't frustrate students by asking them to do things that are too far out of reach or that bore them because they are too easy or repetitive. Respond to different needs in different ways.
Be patient.	Don't cut kids off in conversation. Don't become frustrated when students need more time than anticipated. Don't blame students for not getting it, but patiently look for other ways you can teach it.
Know how to handle frustration.	Use a firm voice with students to communicate frustration, but don't threaten arbitrary consequences or raise your voice. All your actions and words are models.

Position Content Under an Umbrella of Caring

All your hard work, planning, and attention to detail will be lost efforts the moment you lose sight of the child and focus on the work. Yes, your students need reading and writing to thrive and succeed in the world. But your teaching loses its impact when it is based on content before caring. To succeed at high levels, your students need to develop the kind of confidence, independence, and interdependence that can be nurtured only through supportive interactions with caring others. When you successfully position content under an umbrella of caring and connectedness, student outcomes improve.

> **Don't Take My Word for It**
> Research-Based Evidence
>
> In *Visible Learning for Teachers: Maximizing Impact on Learning*, John Hattie (2012) explains that until students feel a sense of safety and connectedness in their classroom, there is little chance they will learn anything of importance: "A positive, caring, respectful climate in the classroom is a prior condition to learning" (70).

Use Books and Conversation to Strengthen the Community

Books, and the conversations they generate, are powerful tools for creating a community of respect, honesty, and risk taking. Books are windows for us to open and explore all kinds of relevant social themes like friendship, honesty, courage, diversity, and forgiveness. Classroom read-alouds and independent reading give your students regular opportunities to safely

* explore who they are and what they are capable of as learners and as people
* take risks and find out what they can stretch themselves to do
* tell others the truth about what really matters to them
* discover and share the things that light them up with joy
* discover and share the things that trigger heartache and tears.

Use Reading Conferences to Support and Understand Individual Students

Using reading conferences to strengthen relationships with individual students pays dividends throughout the school day. In these conversations you can give powerful compliments and feedback that highlight student strengths and self-awareness. You leave each conference knowing more about the child as a reader and a person. A conference is the perfect venue for giving more personal atention to students who are new to the class, who are not making progress, or who lack confidence. Chapter 9 discusses the elements of successful individual conferences.

Fill the Day with Joyful Interactions

Joyful interactions modeled by a joyful teacher are the heart of an engaged classroom. Smile. Have fun. Be enthusiastic. Laugh out loud. Exclaim with joy. Tell kids what you're excited about. Tell kids what they can look forward to. Celebrate sincerely and often. Value students' contributions. Create opportunities for students to interact in meaningful conversations (to learn more about supporting conversation in the reading classroom, see Chapter 10). Feed every child's belief that everyone has something wonderful to offer the learning community you share.

3.2 Teach Expectations with Patience and Consistency

Relationships alone will not turn your students into voracious and engaged readers. They are unlikely to arrive on the first day of school, pick up books, and start reading eagerly and deeply. But they will develop deep engagement over time because you follow these steps:

1. Clearly define your expectations.

2. Turn expectations into habits through patient teaching.

3. Reflect.

4. Monitor and adjust with an eye toward independence.

Clearly Define Your Expectations

Before you can help your students understand your expectations, you'll have to clarify for yourself what you want from them. Picture the good habits you want your students to exhibit when they are reading independently. The answers to the following questions contain important clues to help you figure out what you really want:

* What do I care most deeply about during independent reading?
* What do I want independent reading to look like, sound like, and feel like?
* What do I worry about the most? What can I do to be proactive about it?
* How will I recognize true engagement?
* In what ways will reading in my classroom resemble reading in the real world?

Grab a sheet of paper and scribble down your answers to each of these questions. This is a really important step, so please, please resist the urge to skip it.

Although it may be tempting to leave this long laundry list of expectations as it is, boil your ideas down to five (or fewer) short, action-oriented statements. Look for patterns and categories. If it helps, cut your list apart and move the entries around manually, looking for things that can be grouped together under one umbrella statement. Once you've identified your big categories, state the behavioral expectation for each in clear, simple, positive language. Figure 3.2 shows how one teacher grouped and combined a collection of nitty-gritty expectations into short yet positive expectation statements.

Turn Expectations into Habits Through Patient Teaching

Once you've identified what you expect of students during independent reading, it's time to explain and teach these expectations to your students. Begin by instilling a sense of urgency. *You* understand the importance of lots of reading every day. *You* understand the link between how much one reads and how well one reads. But do your students? Letting them in on the *why* of independent reading helps them develop the same sense of urgency and importance about their daily reading that you feel. Without understanding why so much reading is so important, your students will have a hard time meeting the high expectations you set for them.

Figure 3.2 Creating Short, Positive Expectation Statements

Brainstormed Expectations	Expectations Restated in Positive and Simple Language
No moving around the room. Don't change places. Pick a spot and stick with it.	Stay in your spot.
Start reading right away. Don't dig in your desk. No visiting. No goofing around.	Read the whole time.
Read books you care about. Think about the story. Reread when it doesn't make sense. Try to make connections while reading.	Think while you read.
Try to do your best. Choose books that are a good fit. Try new things. Don't give up.	Work to become a better reader.
Don't disturb others. Read quietly. No pencil sharpening. Don't make fun of what others read.	Be respectful of others.

Potential Teaching Points About Why Daily Reading Matters

* *

  * Reading every day is the best way to become a better reader.
  * The more time you spend with books you *can* read and **want** to read the more you will grow as a reader.
  * Taking time to choose books thoughtfully is an important way to stay engaged.

* *

Figure 3.3 Our Reading Agreements Anchor Chart

As you teach expectations, be careful not to move along too quickly, introducing too many expectations at once without providing enough modeling, support, and practice. Instead, explicitly teach and model each expectation individually over time, showing examples and non-examples of what it looks and sounds like and giving kids ample time to practice and receive clear feedback. *Patient teaching* and *gradual release* are essential when shaping behavior expectations.

Next, you'll want to create an anchor chart with your students to make your expectations visible. Keep sentences short. Leave plenty of white space. Choose a strong visual to support each expectation. (For more about anchor charts, see Chapter 2.) Figure 3.3 shows an example.

Now model, model, and model some more. Modeling is an extremely powerful form of teaching, especially when it comes to expectations. Modeling can be done in a variety of ways:

1. **Show and tell exactly what is expected.** For example, if you want to teach students the proper way to place books back into the library baskets without crunching and damaging pages, don't just tell them; show them. Take them to the library or bring a basket to the rug. Show them the problem (the wrong way) and then show the solution (the correct way) with a precise demonstration and an explanation.

2. **Have a student model the behavior.** This is a great way to give a struggling student an extra chance to shine, although it's a good idea to have a quick practice session in advance. For example, after providing a class demonstration on the correct way to put books away in a basket, Mrs. B. had a quick conference with Alondra, who'd previously had a hard time remembering to be gentle with books. "During our reflection session today, I'd like to remind everyone one more time of the importance of putting books away carefully. I was wondering if you could help me by demonstrating to the class." Alondra's eyes lit up at the prospect; she smiled and nodded. "All right, let's practice, just the two of us, so you'll be ready to demonstrate."

3. **Give students a chance to discuss the modeled behavior with their partners.**
   Because comprehension is enhanced by conversation, you can have students turn
   and talk with their partners (read more about this strategy in Chapter 10) about what
   they've seen: "I want you to think about what you saw Alondra do with her books and
   why it is important. Turn and talk with your elbow partner about the important things
   you noticed."

4. **Use digital photography and video.** If you're looking for ways to make expectations
   more clear and easy to remember, pull out your phone, digital camera, or video camera.
   There are lots of easy ways to use digital technology to enhance this work:

   * Take still shots of students demonstrating the desired behavior and add them to
     your anchor chart.
   * Take photos while students are reading independently and project them during
     that day's sharing session.
   * Ask students to role-play examples of meeting expectations while you
     videotape. Post the videos on the classroom blog.

Reflect

Each day, it's important for both you and your students to reflect on how things are going. To do
this, you'll need to take a few short minutes after independent reading to have a brief conversation focused on three primary questions:

1. What went well today?

2. What was hard today?

3. What do you need to focus on tomorrow?

Taking just a few minutes to reflect on today and plan for tomorrow programs kids' brains
for success. Asking students to process their successes and struggles together allows them to apply
what they know to solve problems and set goals. (You can read more about reflection in Chapter 7.)

Monitor and Adjust with an Eye Toward Independence

The ultimate purpose of defining expectations is to help develop independence. Monitoring
closely helps you understand which expectations are clear to your students and which are not.
Knowing this can help you adjust your instruction accordingly: *Everyone seems to clearly understand
the expectation to start reading right away. I don't need to provide another lesson about that. However, lots
of kids are struggling with reading the whole time. I think I need to shorten the time we spend reading for
a while and teach more strategies related to book selection and engagement.*

Most important, you want to take a problem-solving stance. Don't just say, "If you didn't
read the whole time today, try harder tomorrow." Instead, when you spot a problem, ask yourself, "What could be getting in the way?" If, for example, you believe that reading engagement is
falling apart because students still don't have the optimal combination of good-fit books to hold

their attention, instead of simply scolding them, hold out a nugget of hope: "There is an important connection between good-fit books and engagement. And I'm going to help you consider how finding books that are a better match for you will help you as a reader."

In the end, bringing out the best in your readers depends largely on believing the best of them from the beginning. All students want to succeed. They just need you to patiently help them find their way. Figure 3.4 outlines some questions that will help you help your students read independently.

Step Inside a Classroom

Reflecting on Agreements

Mrs. Wilde's students have come to the gathering space after independent reading. It is the second week of school, and students have been working hard on their first three agreements for independent reading.

"Let's look at our agreements and review them together."

The class does a choral reading of the first three agreements on the anchor chart. "Stay in your own spot. Read the whole time. Be respectful of others."

"I want you to think about the time you spent reading today. In a moment I'll ask you to turn and talk with your partner about our three reflection questions." She points to a chart posted behind her and reads the three questions: "What went well for you today? What was hard for you today? What do you need to focus on tomorrow?" To ensure that students do their own reflection first, she pauses for thirty seconds of silence before she has students begin.

Rachel and Jaden are partners. Rachel begins, "Today the thing that went well was that I stayed in my spot the entire time. I never left it. But I did have a hard time reading the whole time. I was getting sort of bored because I didn't really like any of my books. I'm not sure what I should do better tomorrow. I think it's sort of hard to read the whole entire time."

Jaden immediately replies, "Maybe you need to get better books. Maybe you don't have good-fit books."

Rachel nods. "Maybe. That might be a good idea. I am sort of bored with the ones I picked this time and some of them are too hard." She nods again, still processing the idea. Then, remembering to be a good partner, she says, "How about you? What did you think went well today?"

Figure 3.4 Defining Success for Independent Reading

Helpful Question	Examples	Ideas to Help Students Meet Expectations
What do I want independent reading to look like, sound like, feel like?	Everyone is relaxed but engaged. There is a quiet buzz of reading and conversation about reading. Kids support and encourage each other as readers.	Describe what you want and why. Provide lots of modeling. Look for individual and small-group examples. Make sure you give lots of positive and explicit feedback when kids hit the target, especially when expectations are new. Show a videotape of a successful independent reading session.
What do I care about?	I want kids to really read. I want kids to read only things they care about. I want kids to connect with one another in meaningful ways.	Tell your kids what you want. Define your expectations explicitly. Create anchor charts that highlight essential details. Use visuals to create a lasting image of what you want.
What do I worry might go wrong?	Kids will pretend to read. Kids will waste time doodling or fooling around. Kids will talk about things unrelated to reading.	Have students demonstrate non-examples and then follow up immediately with examples of what you want. Restate expectations. Communicate individually and respectfully with students who are struggling. Consider what you need to reteach so that students meet your expectations. Draw attention to positive examples.
What indicators will I have along the way that I have successfully taught the expectations for independent reading?	There won't be behavior issues. Kids will be logging lots of reading miles. I'll be able to meet with small groups or individuals without being distracted by other students.	Keep a running log of student behavior during independent reading. This will provide clues about what to teach and who needs the instruction. Create a checklist with expectations across the top and a class roster down the side. Document for each student with a simple X or O whether she or he has mastered the expectation. Implement a system by which students can let you know they need your help but are able to keep working while they wait to receive it.

Reflect on Chapter 3

Before moving on, reflect on the quality of both the relationships and the routines in your classroom, remembering that without strong positive relationships, all other learning is at risk. (See Figures 3.5 and 3.6.)

Figure 3.5

Reflection on Relationships

As you consider all the possible ways you might strengthen relationships with individual students in your classroom, which actions will you focus on first?

Figure 3.6

Reflection on Turning Expectations into Routines

Which clear and positively stated expectations for independent reading have you identified?	What next steps will you patiently take to turn these expectations into habits?

FOUR

Provide Choice to Build Engaged and Joyful Readers

The research base on student-selected reading is robust and conclusive: Students read more, understand more, and are more likely to continue reading when they have the opportunity to choose what they read.

—Richard Allington and Rachel E. Gabriel, "Every Child, Every Day"

Coach your students to strengthen reading muscles for engagement and fluency:

1. Give kids choice about what they read, where they read, and how they read (36–41).
2. Cultivate engaged, joyful reading habits (pages 42–46).
3. Stand back and observe (page 47).

Step inside a classroom where real independent reading is happening, and engagement will be easy to spot. Kids will have their noses buried in books. They probably won't have even noticed you walk in. They might be talking with a partner about a book: studying an illustration, sharing a smile, listening intently to each other read aloud, or sharing observations and ideas. They might be quietly jotting thoughts on sticky notes or in response journals. Choice and differentiation will be evident everywhere. Students will be reading books of all kinds: short and long, fiction and nonfiction, leveled and trade, old favorites and brand-new titles. Their reading levels will be diverse and so will be their interests, but one thing will be common to all—their eyes will be on print. Their work will be purposeful and authentic. They'll be engaged.

For such students, reading is joyful, something they look forward to and don't want to miss out on or be pulled away from. Nobody is fake-reading. Nobody's doodling or dawdling. Nobody's talking about recess or after-school plans. Nobody's hiding out at the pencil sharpener or in the restroom. Ownership and success are high; students are on task and know what is expected of them. They're reading—for real!

The suggestions in this chapter will help you build high levels of engagement during independent reading by offering students meaningful choice and control over their reading lives.

4.1 Give Kids Choice About What, Where, and How They Read

Take a moment to think about your own reading habits. If you're like most adults, you read both *because* you choose to read and because of *what* you choose to read. You pick up a newspaper to learn about current events, check on your favorite sports team, or explore topics you are passionate about. You go online to learn more about fly-fishing, training for a marathon, installing a hardwood floor, planning a trip, or understanding the history associated with a local landmark. You read novels dealing with common themes of the human experience. You find authors you love and devour everything they've written. Personal choice drives the majority of your reading.

For too long, however, the majority of students' reading has been assigned. They all read the same passage in the basal reader; they are assigned books for literature circles and book clubs; they read the same class novel at the same pace. None of these experiences prepares students to make authentic and meaningful choices for themselves outside the classroom. Choice is fundamental to both motivation and engagement in the reading classroom. The research supporting choice is clear and decisive.

There are three primary ways to provide choice during independent reading:

1. Let kids choose what they read.

2. Let kids choose where they read.

3. Let kids choose how they read.

Don't Take My Word for It
Research-Based Evidence

When Kids Have Choice, Success and Engagement Levels Rise

In a meta-analysis of twenty-two studies on factors contributing to reading motivation and achievement, Guthrie and Humenick (2004) found that letting students choose what to read, whom to read with, and where to read produced reading gains second only to the gains produced by their having access to interesting texts. Pressley (2003) found lack of student choice a primary factor in undermining motivation and achievement. Children and adults pay closer attention, persist longer, learn more, and show more enjoyment when engaged in topics or activities that focus on their individual interests (Hidi and Harackiewicz 2000).

Choosing What to Read

Kids need to choose most of their independent reading. Chapter 6 will help you guide your stu
dents to become increasingly skilled at selecting books that they *can* and *want to* read. For now,
let them know you want them to choose books they *care about* and *can read*. Even if they do it
imperfectly (and rest assured, some of them will), remember that learning to do anything well
requires some missteps along the way. Choice is powerful even when imperfect.

In the beginning, don't worry too much when your students choose texts you think are too
hard or too easy. Eventually, because of your patient teaching and support, they'll learn to make
more refined choices, but you can't teach them everything at once. Figure 4.1 lists ways you can
support good book choices in the early days of independent reading.

Figure 4.1 Suggestions for Supporting Early Book Choice

Supporting Early Book Choice	
Teach three ways to read a book (see Chapter 6 for details).	By teaching three ways to read a book, you reassure your students that you will accept a range of approaches to early reading, including 1. Reading the pictures. 2. Retelling the story. 3. Reading the words. These three ways to read a book are especially helpful as K–1 students and students with very limited English develop independence.
Trust your kids.	Always approach book choice with a spirit of optimism and trust. Believe your kids have the best of intentions when choosing books.
Patiently respect their early book choices.	Learning to choose appropriate books takes time and practice, trial and error, explicit teaching and reinforcement. It is one of the most important life skills for readers to have. Resist the urge to correct students' less-than-perfect choices too quickly; book selection is a developing skill.
Provide ongoing teaching.	Your students will need ongoing teaching about how readers consistently make good choices, delivered during whole-class instruction, small-group instruction, and individual conferences.
Avoid being too rigid about levels.	Although reading levels are very important for instructional purposes, kids need the freedom both to stretch themselves with more difficult material and to revisit simpler materials during independent reading. When they are motivated by choice, kids are often capable of more than we imagine.

Step Inside a Classroom

Finding Books They Want to Read from Day One

On the first day of school, Mrs. Taylor gathers her children on the rug in the meeting area. In her lap is a basket of books of a variety of shapes, sizes, and genres. They are some of her favorites, chosen to help her demonstrate her absolute love of books, a love she wants to inspire in each of her students this year. There are lots of independent reading routines and procedures she'll need to teach in the coming days, but her first priority is to instill a sense of joy and anticipation about the journey ahead.

"Readers, this is going to be an amazing year! Every single day you are going to go on adventures, meet new and fascinating people, learn about things you really care about, and just plain have fun because every single day you'll spend some time reading about things *you* choose, things *you* care about, things *you* want to read.

"This year, I'm putting *you* in charge of choosing the books you want to read to help you grow as a reader and a person. You'll be in charge of what adventures to take and what learning to focus on through the books you choose. You'll discover all kinds of new possibilities for reading by exploring topics, authors, and genres. To get started, think back on some of the best things you've read in the past."

Students turn and talk with partners about topics, genres, or authors they've loved in the past. This gets kids thinking about their own successes as readers and gives Mrs. Taylor a quick first glimpse into the past reading lives they've had and the texts she might gather or highlight during the coming days:

* ✱ "I mostly like to read about science—experiments and stuff. I have this really cool book at home with 101 science experiments, and we did a bunch of them this summer."
* ✱ "I love mysteries. Last year I read every A to Z Mysteries book in the library. I like trying to figure it out before the end."
* ✱ "I don't really like reading that much. Mostly I only read the books the teacher tells me I have to. My mom says my brother is the bookworm in the family and I'm the social one."
* ✱ "Sports. Baseball and football especially. They had great sports books at the book fair last year and I got this one about famous quarterbacks."
* ✱ "The Diary of a Wimpy Kid books are my favorite. I wish there were even more of them."

Next Mrs. Taylor says, "Readers, later we'll choose books from our classroom library and the school library. But today, let's start our reading journey by exploring the amazing books in the baskets on each of the tables. I hope as you browse through these baskets you'll find one or two books you'd like to spend more time with." The baskets contain a range of reading levels, topics, genres, and especially lots of nonfiction with rich photography and engaging text features, and she is confident students will find books they'll be eager to explore.

Choosing Where to Read

Most adult readers have favorite reading spots and routines. Most adults don't read a novel sitting upright at a desk (although a few may). Some seek a comfortable chair in a quiet, out-of-the-way place. Others want to be right in the middle of things.

Kids are no different. All sorts of spaces support their independent reading. Some students have a very clear idea of the space that works for them, and you will try to accommodate them. Others haven't done enough sustained independent reading to know yet; they'll need your patience and maybe your help as they try things out.

I'm not suggesting that anything goes, but you need to stretch your thinking about what appeals to and works for kids. Appendix B (available online at www.heinemann.com/products /E06155.aspx) provides a list of possible reading spots. As you consider the list, ask yourself, "Am I comfortable offering this as an option to my students?"

After identifying spots you're comfortable with, you may want to make a map of your classroom showing these spots (see Figure 4.2). This ensures there are enough appealing and appropriate spots for everyone, shows students what choices are available, and lets you keep track of

Figure 4.2 Classroom Reading Sports Map

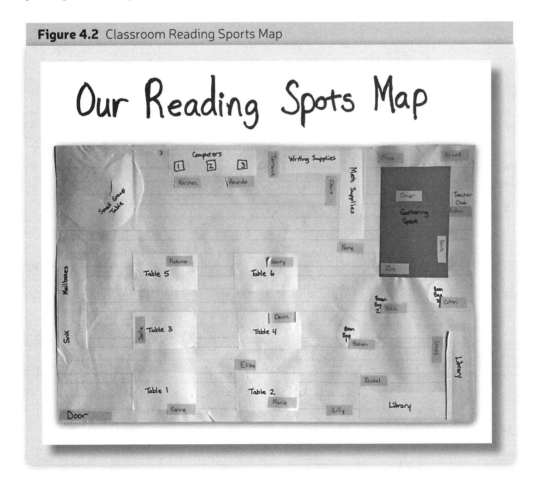

who reads where. As students choose their spots, put sticky notes labeled with their names on the map. The sticky notes are easy to change as students move around. (When both you and your students are more comfortable with independent reading, you may no longer need the map.)

To begin, have kids stay with their chosen spots for two or three weeks at a time, then try out new spots. If a particular space isn't working for a student, help that child find one where he or she can work productively. If you can do this without triggering frustration or creating a power struggle (see Figure 4.3), the student will be much more likely to accept the new spot and flourish there.

Choosing How to Read

Readers read in a variety of ways. You can offer students some simple starting points about how to read the books they've chosen: (1) utilize three ways to read a book (for early readers); (2) reread; and (3) reconsider.

UTILIZE THREE WAYS TO READ A BOOK

Emergent and early readers need to know the three ways to read a book; retell, read the pictures, or read the words (described in more detail in Chapter 6). This gives them options for interacting with a variety of picture books, many of which are too difficult to read word for word but can still provide rich experiences in oral storytelling, sequencing, and cognition.

Figure 4.3 Teacher Language to Support the Choice of Suitable Reading Spots

Language to Help Students Find Suitable Reading Spots

Instead of saying . . .	Try something like . . .	Because . . .
I can see this spot isn't working for you.	I'm wondering what you're thinking about this spot. Does it feel like you've found the right spot?	It empowers the student and calls on her or him to be reflective.
If you can't stay focused, I'm going to have to move you.	Maybe something about this spot is making it hard for you to focus. What do you think? Let's try it for another day, and if it doesn't get easier, let's work together to find a different spot.	It empowers the student but sets a specific time for exploring other options.
You're going to have to move back to your desk. You aren't able to handle it on the floor.	I've been thinking about a couple of other options that might make it easier for you to stay focused during independent reading—reading in the corner over by the computer table or enclosing your desk with a cardboard office. Which of those would you like to try?	It allows you to move the student to a different spot while still offering some level of authentic choice.

REREAD

Your students need to know that when they are reading independently, rereading is an acceptable—even smart—thing that real readers do. Whether they do it for sheer enjoyment or to understand more deeply, all readers find rereading a valuable strategy. Rereading a book is a sign of a deep connection with the text. However, if you suspect that a student's rereading is not a productive choice, you might start a conversation about it.

Instead of saying . . .	Try something like . . .
You've already read that book. Choose something different.	I notice you're choosing to reread this book. What can you tell me about how you made that choice?

RECONSIDER

If I were forced to go back and finish every book I've started, I'd likely have to trade in a year or more of my life to do so. Smart readers, even after working hard to make smart book selections, sometimes change their minds about a book after starting it. Time in the reading classroom (and in life) is too valuable to be wasted on texts that don't fit. Our students need permission to try a book out, change their minds, and abandon the book. They also need permission to read only *some* parts of a book, especially an informational text.

Changing Their Minds Too Often

Although you want students to know it's OK sometimes to change their minds about a book, some kids become chronic book abandoners, jumping quickly from one not-so-great choice to another. Digging a bit deeper, you'll often find they are choosing books that are too difficult in the first place. These students most likely *don't* need to be pressured to stick with their current choice until the end. What they do need is help with making a good choice in the first place. When you work closely with them to select a book they are interested in and can read, the likelihood they will stick with it will go way up. Being aware of their interests and reading level is essential in helping these students make better choices.

Instead of saying . . .	Try something like . . .
This time you need to stick with your book from beginning to end.	I notice you're having some trouble finding books that you want to stick with to the end. I'm wondering whether the books you're choosing are truly right for you. I'd like work with you on your next book choice to find one you really want to stick with. Are you open to some help?

4.2 Cultivate Engaged, Joyful Reading Habits for All

When students aren't able to stay focused while reading independently, it is easy to blame *them*. They're fooling around. They don't care about reading. They're naughty. They want attention. But even the trickiest kids can stay engaged if you view their struggles through the lens of how you can help them improve. All students can become more engaged readers if we encourage them in the four ways listed below.

Four Ways to Support Higher Levels of Reading Engagement

1. Be patient.

2. Examine what kids are reading.

3. Examine their reading spots.

4. Set a goal or make a plan that includes breaks.

Be Patient

Building reading muscles takes time. Anyone who has gotten better at anything did so because she or he stuck with it, even when it was tricky.

Examine What They Are Reading

Book fit is the first and last place to look when considering what might be preventing students from staying engaged during independent reading. As you think about book fit, consider the following:

* **Is the student interested?** If not, have him or her consider a different book. This doesn't necessarily mean abandoning the first book (although sometimes it will). Instead, it means that some days certain kinds of reading are more appealing and manageable than others. Adults often have several books going at once, moving between them based on interest, purpose, and mood. Kids need permission to do that as well. A student who has been reading a Mercy Watson for three days in a row may approach independent reading eager to dig in and continue. On the other hand, he may be thinking about soccer tryouts after school and be more interested in his book about soccer.

* **Is the book too easy or too difficult?** Reading books that are too difficult or too easy makes it hard to stay focused. This doesn't mean students should never choose those books. But you want students to be aware of the choices they are making. When a student is motivated to struggle through a challenging book, it may not affect engagement. But if she is feeling frustrated by a challenging book, focus will undoubtedly suffer. Teach kids to ask themselves, "Am I having a hard time staying focused because my book choice is too hard? Too easy?"

✱ **Do they have enough books?** Although older students may need only one chapter book to carry them through a day of independent reading, younger readers need a lot of books in their buckets or bags. Figure 4.4 suggests the number of books kids need in each of the grades.

Figure 4.4 Possible Book Box Contents by Grade

Kindergarten	First Grade	Second Grade	Third–Fifth Grades
✱ 8–10 books at independent level ✱ 2–3 familiar books for retelling ✱ 2 more complex high-interest nonfiction books for "reading" the pictures	✱ 8–12 books at independent level ✱ 2–4 more complex high-interest books	✱ 1–2 chapter books at independent level ✱ 3–4 picture books ✱ 4–6 nonfiction books	✱ 1 chapter book ✱ 1 nonfiction book ✱ 1 picture book or poetry book

Examine Their Reading Spots

Sometimes staying focused is more difficult because the reading spot is not a good match with the student's needs. Consider the following:

✱ **Is the child comfortable?** Focus depends on comfort. If a student is hunched over in an awkward position, he or she is more likely to wiggle and squirm than if he or she is sitting in a comfortable position with the back and body well supported. What's comfortable for one student is not necessarily comfortable for all, but comfort is an important consideration for everyone.

✱ **Does the student have enough space?** Being too close to other people or distracting situations can make it difficult to stay engaged. When a student is struggling to stay focused, encourage the student to think about the space she or he has chosen: is there anything about it that could be improved? (See Chapters 1 and 2 for more ideas about helping kids find spots that work.)

Set a Goal or Make a Plan That Includes Breaks

Students who need additional support to stay engaged may need a slightly different routine from the rest of the class. Some readers benefit from a schedule that alternates reading with other activities. For instance, a child may plan to read one short leveled book and then stop to sketch a picture about it on a sticky note. Alternating between reading and writing makes it easier for the student to stay engaged. Students who need to move around may want to take a short walk between books or chapters. Figure 4.5 suggests simple options for the few readers in your classroom who need special accommodations in order to match the stamina of their peers.

Figure 4.5 Take-a-Break Options for Restless Readers

Option	How It Works
Rest stop	The student places a bookmark or sticky note a certain number of pages ahead. When she reaches that spot, she takes a short break using one of the options here and then returns to independent reading.
Stop and jot	The student stops at designated spots and jots a note or draws a sketch on a sticky note about what he's read.
Picture it	After reading the designated number of pages, chapters, or books, the student moves to a work area and draws a picture using a full-size sheet of paper and crayons or markers.
This book, that book	A child reads a designated number of pages, chapters, or books and then is able to spend time with a favorite "look book"—a nonfiction book with lots of pictures and drawings or a novelty book such as an I Spy or Where's Waldo? book.
Walk this way	The child takes a walk—to the drinking fountain, up and down the hallway, to a window and back—when he has read the designated number of pages.

It's important to remember that you're not building stamina for stamina's sake but to support reading engagement. If kids are going to do a great deal of daily independent reading, they must be able to stay focused for long stretches of time. Most often, students who don't have reading stamina are not yet deeply and joyfully engaged readers. However, for every disengaged reader there is a potential solution. Figure 4.6 suggests ways to help various types of disengaged readers. Figure 4.7 contains a number of questions you can ask yourself about students who are not able to stay engaged with reading.

Figure 4.6 Strategies for Helping Disengaged Readers

Type of Reader	Descriptors	How to Help
Fake-it reader	Pretends to read Turns pages frequently Looks around the room May wander around the room Is rarely excited about reading	Use conferences, check-ins, and surveys to find out why the student doesn't read and what might interest him or her. Be patient and persistent in finding a hook into reading.
Reading-is-hard reader	Reads below grade level Has struggled for a long time and is starting to give up May have learning or language challenges	Determine the student's reading level and interests. Match the child with good-fit books and monitor her or his reading closely. Finding a series the child is excited about and is able to read can be a lifesaver.
Keeping-up-with-the-Joneses reader	Often chooses books that are not a good match and are too difficult Abandons books when she or he gets frustrated Always seems to be starting a new book	Use inventories to determine the student's interests. Introduce books appropriate for the child in whole-class book talks (this type of student wants to read what the rest of the kids are reading). During conferences, focus on choosing books the reader is able to stick with and strategies for when reading gets tough.
Because-you-say-so reader	Reads because you tell him he has to Rarely falls in love with a book Doesn't read outside class	Be enthusiastic about books. Sell the love of reading. Create a classroom in which books are valued and students talk about reading and get excited when new books arrive. Provide great books and help the students choose ones that are a good fit.

Adapted from "Facilitating Engagement by Differentiating Independent Reading," by Kelley and Clausen-Grace (2009).

Figure 4.7 Problem-Solving Questions and Possible Solutions for Increasing Engagement

Question	Possible Solution
Do students have enough books?	Sometimes the youngest readers don't have enough materials in their baskets to keep them engaged. Evaluate the quantity and variety of books in each child's reading basket.
Do they have enough books they really want to read?	The books they have might not be interesting. Make sure there are lots of great choices in your library.
Do they have enough books at the appropriate reading level?	The books might be too challenging or too easy. Continue to teach and support students in finding good-fit books.
Do they have a regular schedule for replenishing their books?	They might be bored with their books. Make sure they get some fresh books at least once a week.
Have I helped them build stamina gradually over time?	Moving too quickly to long chunks of reading can make it difficult for kids. Build slowly and gradually over time.
Have I identified and modeled effective routines and expectations?	Unless students are crystal clear about what is expected, they will not be able to deliver. Post your expectations on an anchor chart. Reteach and modify them as necessary.
Have I safeguarded independent reading against other activities?	If students read independently only occasionally, or if you are distracted by other things while they are reading, it is unlikely they will remain engaged for long periods day after day. Protect independent reading with the ferociousness of a mama lion protecting her cubs.
Have I built in time to reflect and plan at the end of the day?	Readers need time to reflect on how things are going every day. Make sure your students have it.
Do I periodically observe my readers and reflect on what they need next?	It's easy to assume you know exactly what's happening in your classroom and what your readers need. But unless you step back and observe objectively, you may miss important information. When readers are struggling, you need to know why in order to help them.
Do I regularly confer with individual readers?	Conferences help you understand individual reader's choices, skills, and struggles so you can coach and plan accordingly. One-to-one time with you is essential to the success of every one of your readers.

Stand Back and Observe

The truth about independent reading is that there is not one scripted and precise formula for engagement. *You* are the best judge of what your kids need. So, you'll want to make a habit of studying your readers and thinking reflectively about what they need next:

* What is going well for some students? All students?
* What seems hard for some students? All students?
* What will be most important to focus on teaching or reinforcing for all students? Some students?

Stepping back to study your readers is easy. You can start on the very first day of independent reading by simply learning to watch your students read through the eyes of a curious outsider. Notice what goes well and not so well. Then make some notes. There is a simple two-column tool you may find helpful in Appendix E (available online at www.heinemann.com/products /E06155.aspx). In the first column, write down what is going well or things you want to celebrate. In the second column, write down what you want to teach your students next.

The trickiest part will be resisting the urge to interrupt and redirect every time you see something go wrong. Instead, jot it down in the right-hand column. Try to stay detached: you're going to address the things that require more instruction, just not right this minute. Then each day, select one powerful thing to help your students with next and teach it in the minutes just prior to independent reading (you'll learn more about the minilesson in Chapter 7). You can't teach everything at once, and you don't want to give up too much of the valuable reading time you worked so hard to find, so limit your teaching point to *one* short and powerful nugget.

Be sure to look for things to celebrate as well. Make a note of these and end each day by publicly acknowledging the specific reading behavior you observed that you hope to see repeated. Celebration lets kids know you don't notice just off-task behavior; you also notice effective reading behavior.

Reflect on Chapter 4

Your students won't show up ready to read for long stretches of uninterrupted time with high levels of engagement. But you can get them there, with time and commitment. The kids who need you most are probably those that need the most time *and* most patience. They're lucky to have you. Reflect on the goals for this chapter and select a few simple action steps (see Figure 4.8).

Figure 4.8 Chapter 4 Reflections and Plans

The Goals	Reflections and Plans
Providing choice. I'm ready to let my kids choose because I understand the relationship between choice and engagement. I am ready to trust and nurture my students' ability to make choices about what to read, where to read, and how to read.	
Patient problem solving and planning. I'm committed to the readers who need me most. I'm patiently working to help increase their levels of engagement.	
Studying readers. I regularly stand back and study my readers; I think about what is going well and what I might teach in the future. I have a system for taking notes about my observations.	

FIVE

Build Efficient Classroom Library Routines

Think about the last time you went to the library or bookstore, or even looked for a book on Amazon online. The process of finding a book takes time. The children in our classrooms are no different. They need time to browse books in order to find a good fit.

—Gail Boushey and Joan Moser, *The Daily 5*

Make shopping in the classroom library a successful routine for all students:

1. Teach students to treat books with respect and care (pages 50–53).
2. Establish when the library is open for business and when it is not (pages 54–56).
3. Teach students to find what they're looking for in the classroom library (pages 56–61).

Get Your Students on Board

"Aren't books amazing and wonderful things? And aren't we lucky to have a whole big collection of them right here in our classroom? Our classroom library is going to be a great and ready resource for us this year as we keep reading, reading, and reading. If we work together, we'll be able to protect the books from getting damaged, keep them organized in ways that everyone can find them, and work out a plan so everyone gets to spend the time she or he needs there to find great books."

Picture your students moving smoothly in and out of the library, exclaiming with joy at the books they've found. Sound appealing but impossible? It's not. You can get there by designing book-shopping routines that ensure students in your classroom don't have to give up precious reading minutes to find books they are excited to read independently.

Once you commit to having your kids do a large amount of independent reading every day, it won't be long before you wonder how you'll get enough great books in your kids' hands to keep them engaged as readers for big chunks of time each day. Finding books worth reading takes time, and teaching students to navigate the classroom library requires the same kind of explicit, patient teaching that other classroom routines do. It begins with you in the library, modeling and explaining exactly what to do, and moves gradually toward student independence. (To learn more about teaching expectations and routines, see Chapter 3.)

 ## 5.1 Teach Students to Treat Books with Respect and Care

Before you turn your students loose in the classroom library, you need to make sure they know how much you value and treasure this precious book collection. Let them know that you'll need their help safeguarding the books from being handled roughly, having their pages bent, being written in, and being placed carelessly in baskets. Kathy Collins (2008) suggests that when you spot books being mistreated early in the year, you react dramatically in front of the whole class:

> *Oh, my word. I can't believe what I see. Someone must have dropped a book*
> *on the counter right next to the paint cups without realizing it. I am so*
> *relieved that it has not gotten paint or water on it. If you ever see a book*
> *that has been carelessly left in a place where it could be damaged, please help*
> *take care of the book by putting it safely back in our library. I'm really going*
> *to need your help with this so we can protect all of our books from damage.*

A powerful think-aloud like this paired with a demonstration of how to treat books respectfully helps students understand how seriously you want them to take their role of book protectors. Figure 5.1 suggests other things you might teach students about the careful handling of books.

> *These books are like treasures, and we need to take care of each one of them*
>
> —Kathy Collins, *Growing Readers: Units of Study in the Primary Classroom*

As you teach book-handling skills early in the year, create an anchor chart and post it in your classroom library as reference and reminder. (See the example in Figure 5.2. Read more about anchor charts in Chapter 2.)

Figure 5.1 Ideas for Teaching Students to Respect and Care for Books

What You Might Teach	Why It Matters
Keep books in your book bag or basket.	Without clear direction, kids are prone to leave books lying around or, worse yet, stuff them into their desks. Sometimes books get left on the floor, where they are inevitably stepped on, or too close to something wet, where they inevitably get waterlogged.
Use a bookmark.	This is an alternative to folding a page over to mark your spot. Although we sometimes turn down the pages of books we own ourselves, this is not appropriate for shared collections.
Use sticky notes.	Although adults sometimes make notes in their own books, this is obviously not appropriate for the shared library collections at school. Sticky notes are a great way to leave "thinking tracks" without harming the books.
Place books in the front of the library baskets.	When books get shoved into the middle of a basket, the pages often get rumpled and tangled. Teaching students to slide books into the front of a basket applies to both individual book boxes and library baskets.
Leave some wiggle room in the library baskets.	When baskets get overcrowded, both the books and the baskets are likely to be damaged. Teach kids not to overstuff baskets by showing several examples of too much and just right.
Return books when you're finished.	You've seen it. Some kids leave a trail of books behind them everywhere they go. Teach students to be good stewards of the shared collection by not keeping more books than they really need and promptly returning them to the shared collection when they're done, so others can enjoy them too.

Figure 5.2 Book Care Anchor Chart

Step Inside a Classroom

Book Shopping in Kindergarten

It's center time in Mrs. Green's classroom. Children are happily building with blocks, exploring art supplies, acting out a story. Mrs. Green is sitting on the floor in the classroom library with the four students from the Tuesday book-shopping group. The children have their individual book tubs with them and are going to trade ten of the twelve books for new ones.

First, Mrs. Green asks them to choose their two very favorite books from the past week to keep this week. The students buzz with excitement as they chat about which books they loved last week, in essence giving mini book talks. Ultimately they each select two books for their I-love-you-so-much-I'm-going-to-keep-you-for-another-week award. Mrs. Green knows this kind of critical thinking is good for kids, as is the empowerment they feel from having some familiar anchors in their book box each week. The kids love finding and announcing which books they deem to be best.

"I'm keeping *Cookies Week*, for sure," Josiah says, without hesitating.

"I'm keeping *Brown Bear*, because my baby brother loves it when I read it to him," Zoe announces.

Once they've each selected their favorites to keep, Mrs. Green helps them stack their remaining eight books neatly and begin to put them away, matching the stickers on the backs of the books with the stickers on the fronts of the library book bins. She has taught kids to handle books as though they are prized possessions and gives gentle reminders of this when needed.

* **Some of the books have stars on the back.** These are books, several copies of each, that Mrs. Green has read aloud and that the kindergartners can retell with zeal and success. These books go back in a star basket.

* **Some of the books have colored dots on the back.** These colors correspond to a range of readability levels: the red dots are levels A and B; the blue dots are C and D; and so on. Based on what she knows about her readers, Mrs. Green has helped them determine their special dot color, which changes throughout the year.

* **Some books have stickers with words and pictures.** These books are sorted by topic in the library. Mrs. Green's topic bins have a mixture of fiction and

nonfiction. For example, there is a basket of bear books that has stories and informational books, a basket reserved for Biscuit books, and a basket for Laura Numeroff books.

When all the books have been carefully put away, Mrs. Green reminds the children of their own special dot colors and has them take those bins off the shelf and start looking through them, searching for at least five books they want to keep for the coming week. (The group is made up of shoppers at a range of reading levels, so everyone isn't looking through the same bin at the same time.)

"Claire, what are you finding?" Mrs. Green asks.

"I wanted another Bella and Rosie book," Claire says, flipping through the green basket, "but I can't see one. Hey, Baby Bear! I had a Baby Bear book last time."

"Claire is looking for more books about favorite characters she's enjoyed reading about in the past," Mrs. Green says, simultaneously reaffirming Claire and reminding the others of this smart book-selection strategy.

After students have chosen books at their readability level, they select at least three star books and three interesting books from the topical bins. Some students will be able to read the words in these books, but many will retell the stories and "read" the pictures.

"Hey, a soccer book!" Mason exclaims, pulling it out. "I already started soccer so this is a great book for me."

"Mason, you're thinking about what interests you as you shop for books," Mrs. Green says, reinforcing his efforts.

As the children shop, Mrs. Green continues to encourage them to talk about their choices: "Tell me how you decided on that one." "Wow! What has you so excited about that choice?" From time to time she singles out certain books, opening them up and pointing out a funny character or an interesting diagram. After all the children have selected their books, she asks each student to choose the book he or she is most excited to read, show it to the group, and put it in the front of the bin so the child will be ready to read it immediately. Energy is high; the excitement of exploring new books is obvious.

Before their shopping excursion ends, the children take a careful look around the library to make sure everything is shipshape and ready for tomorrow's shoppers.

5.2 Establish When the Library Is Open for Business and When It Is Not

No matter what grade you teach, you'll need to decide when your classroom library is open and when it's not. When your students are new to classroom library routines, you'll want the library open during times when you are able to provide support and supervision. This will ensure that your students establish good habits from the start. (See Figure 5.3.)

Although independent reading may seem a logical opportunity to let students browse in the library, that's the one time it will usually be off-limits. You want your students to read when they're supposed to be reading and shop for books when they're supposed to be shopping. When book shopping is an option during independent reading, some kids will choose shopping *instead of* reading:

* **A few of them are I'll-do-anything-to-avoid-reading kids.** Especially if reading feels hard or uncomfortable, hanging out in the library and flipping through books is a clever escape. It makes you look like a reader without ever having to read a word.
* **A few of them are I-love-books-so-much-I-can't-settle-on-just-one kids.** These kids could hang out in the library happily contemplating books all day long. (A bit like me trying to decide what to order from an extensive menu illustrated with mouth-watering pictures. I need the people I'm dining with to tell the waitress we're ready to order or I might never decide!)
* **A few of them are social kids.** When they see a few of their friends gathered in the library, all they can think about is how much they want to be there, too. Socialization is good for kids, and talking about books is good for kids—but not when they're happening instead of reading.

Kids can shop for books when they arrive in the morning, during morning routines, while eating their snack, during a free-choice period, or during small-group reading instruction.

Ideally, your library will sometimes be open for everyone and at other times only for specific students on a designated once-a-week schedule. Students' goal on their weekly shopping trip is to select enough books to last the entire week, but they don't need to read fresh material every day. In fact, primary-grade students will reread the same book many times. This not only makes managing the number of books easier but also is one of the best ways for young children to develop fluency, expression, intonation, and confidence as readers. Determining shopping times and small-group schedules that work for you and your students may take some experimentation. Just make a start and adjust as you go.

Figure 5.3 Classroom Library Hours Anchor Chart

Step Inside a Classroom

Book Shopping in Second Grade

During the first fifteen minutes each morning, Mrs. Kennedy's classroom is bustling. Students enter the room with purpose and urgency: being ready for the morning meeting at 8:40 is an important classroom goal. After placing their homework folders in the proper basket and indicating their lunch choices on the whiteboard, students check the daily assignment board. Some see their names next to classroom jobs (water the plants, sharpen the pencils, check off the homework folders, etc.). Others find it's their day to shop for new books in the library. Students without a specific assignment work on an illustration to support their work in writing workshop, read a book, or visit quietly with a classmate about either their writing project or a book they are reading.

Mrs. Kennedy greets students, takes care of clerical tasks, and periodically stops by the library to see how book selection is going for today's shoppers. "I didn't know we got new Mo Willems books," Hattie says, as she flips through the New Additions basket.

"Yes," Mrs. Kennedy says, "I thought of you because I know how you love Elephant and Piggie books."

"I can't believe they're still here," Hattie says. (These popular books are some of the first to leave the library.)

"It's your lucky day," Mrs. Kennedy says, smiling.

Although the library in Mrs. Kennedy's classroom is always open during free-choice periods and when students have completed their work, her class of twenty-five students is divided into five shopping groups, numbered 1 through 5, and one group shops each day. A formally assigned shopping schedule helps Mrs. Kennedy ensure that nobody shows up for independent reading without enough books to read.

Although there are five groups, Mrs. Kennedy doesn't label them by day of the week: she's tired of rescheduling groups on weekdays when there is no school. She posts the shopping group numbers on a big sign above the library with an arrow that says "Today's shopping group is . . ." Each day she rotates the arrow sequentially. Kids enter the room in the morning and check whether it's their group's turn to shop.

Because second graders are reading books within a wide range of difficulty levels and lengths, they aren't all ready to trade all their books every week, as they did in kindergarten. Mrs. Kennedy has taught them some rules of thumb for shopping, which are posted on an anchor chart in the classroom library:

continues

- ✕ Always look for good-fit books. Remember the three-finger rule. (You can read more about this strategy in Chapter 6.)
- ✕ Keep the books you love so much you want to read them again.
- ✕ Keep the books you haven't finished reading.
- ✕ Choose two informational books, one on a topic you love and one on a topic that is less familiar.
- ✕ Choose two fiction books. If one is a chapter book, choose a picture book as well.
- ✕ Check out lots of different bins.
- ✕ Get suggestions from your classmates.

Because learning to select appropriate books independently is an important skill for second graders, Mrs. Kennedy lets her students have plenty of space and autonomy when they are shopping for books. She is prepared for kids to make a few not-so-great selections and knows that these choices can inform her future instruction. For her, helping students choose the right books is a patient, yearlong process.

At the beginning of the year, she met with small groups in the library and helped them with book selection. Now these kids are much more proficient and independent, and she relies on periodic check-ins during each morning's group shopping expedition. When she discovers individual students who are struggling, she strengthens their skills during a one-to-one conference. If several students need the same kind of support (placing books back in baskets facing forward, previewing books to consider their fit, reading a few pages to check for readability, etc.), she works with these readers during a small-group meeting in the library. If routines need to be retaught to many students or modified, she does this during whole-class instruction.

5.3 Teach Students to Find What They're Looking For

After all the hard work you've put into designing and organizing your classroom library, you still need to teach students how it is organized. Although it's obvious to you that all books on the top shelf are leveled readers, books on the second shelf are informational, and books on the bottom shelf are fiction, it may not be obvious to your students. If you want students to be able to find books efficiently, they need to know how things are organized. Some teachers create a diagram of the classroom library that students keep in their reading notebooks; others post a larger version in the library. It can be as simple as a grid depicting the shelves or baskets in the library (see Figure 5.4) and should be easy to update as the library changes throughout the year.

Figure 5.4 Diagram of a Classroom Library

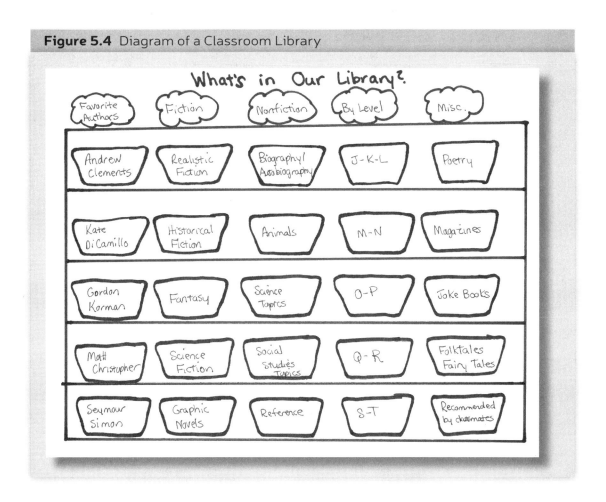

Regardless of their age or reading level, your students will need guidance, or rules of thumb, for selecting books. Some teachers print small cards—shopping lists, in essence—for their students to take with them when they visit the classroom library. The example in Figure 5.5, for first graders, allows both general guidance and individualization. This teacher uses basket colors to differentiate broad categories in her classroom library—all nonfiction is in blue baskets; favorite authors and series are in orange baskets. She can give all students the same guidance in some categories (everyone shops for two nonfiction books)

Figure 5.5 First-Grade Book-Shopping Card

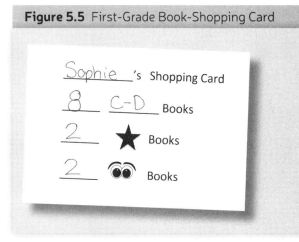

Figure 5.6 Book Box Contents Anchor Chart

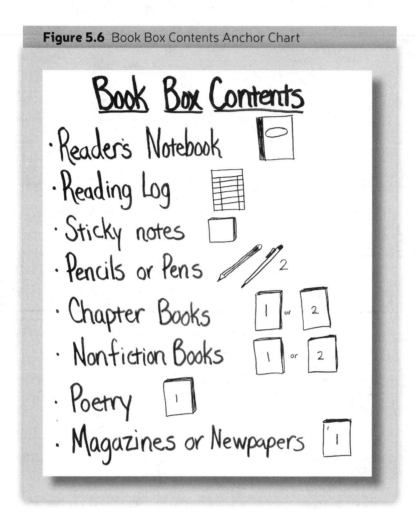

and individualize other categories (students reading at lower levels need more just-right books because the books are so much shorter).

A shopping card also allows you to guide students to focus more heavily on different types of texts during certain times of year. For example, when teaching a unit on nonfiction, you probably want the majority of students' reading material to be informational books; when teaching a unit on characterization, you want to make sure everyone selects strong fiction. Older students can rely on an anchor chart to help them find the right variety of texts to keep in their book boxes. The anchor chart in Figure 5.6 is an example. The numbers for each type of text can easily be changed with a sticky note.

As kids get older, more time can elapse between when they first discover a book and when they read it. In the intermediate grades, you'll want to provide a form on which students can keep a running list of books they've learned about through book talks, book trailers, conversations, or other recommendations and are considering reading in the future (see Figure 5.7).

Figure 5.7 Possible Future Reads

Possible Future Reads	
Title /Author	**Notes** **(Where did I learn about the book?** **What else do I want to remember?)**
Almost Home Joan Bauer	I love the author
Tales of a 4th grade nothing Judy Blue	2nd book in series reminds me of Otherwise known as Sheila the Great
Are you there God it's me, Margret Judy Blume	I love the author
What happened on Fox Street Trisha Springstub	book talk sounds funny
Becoming Naomi Leon Pam muñoz Ryan	Lydia recommended it
The one and only Ivan Katherine Applegate	She loved it! sound really good
When you reach me Rebecca Stead	book trailer looks awesome
A single Shard Linda Sue Park	book talk looks wonderful!!!
Mockingbird Katherine Erskine	Mrs.S recommended it sounds sort of like rules she has autism

Step Inside a Classroom

Book Shopping in Fourth Grade

Mrs. Shale's schedule is tight. With so many curricular areas to teach and so much urgency to get her students ready for middle school, she needs to use every minute efficiently. With no formal breaks in her day other than recess, lunch, and special classes, she needs to be creative to keep book shopping from interfering with independent reading.

Because her fourth graders are reading longer informational texts and chapter books, they don't require as many books to keep them going. But one thing Mrs. Shale wants to avoid at all costs is having students waste time during independent reading because they are between books and don't know what to read next. Therefore, she has worked diligently to instill in them a next-reads mind-set. She's taught them to think beyond *this book* and continually look for and record future possibilities. She relies on book talks, book trailers, and other forms of recommendations to prompt every student to keep a list of next reads in his or her reading notebook.

Her kids have reading tubs, but Mrs. Shale refers to these tubs as *reading shelves*. The analogy helps her students envision reading lives beyond the classroom. Each child's reading shelf contains

- one or two books the student is currently reading
- one or two books the student plans to read in the future
- at least one novel, one picture book, and one informational book
- a reading notebook (which includes a reading log, a list of future reads, minilesson teaching points, and the reader's response entries)
- sticky notes
- writing utensils.

An anchor chart reminding students of the many options they have for selecting new books hangs above the classroom library:

When can I get new books?

- during class visits to the school library
- after I've checked in in the morning
- during the catch-up period at the end of the day
- during a book-selection conference
- during a "great books" group meeting.

During class visits to the school library. Twice a week, Mrs. Shale's fourth graders visit the school library, stocking their reading shelves from this resource as well. Students know how to join a waiting list for a book they want that is currently checked out by someone else. Mrs. Shale and the school librarian work closely together, sharing complementary strategies for helping students find a steady stream of interesting books.

After I've checked in in the morning. The classroom library is always open the first ten or fifteen minutes of the day while students are checking in. Students are not scheduled to shop on any particular day but decide for themselves when they need to visit.

During the catch-up period at the end of the day. To prepare them for middle school, Mrs. Shale gives her students fifteen minutes at the end of the day to work on unfinished tasks and plan their homework. Students can spend time in the library during this period.

During a book-selection conference. At the back of the room Mrs. Shale keeps a strip of laminated tagboard that reads, "I need a book-selection conference." Any student who is struggling to find a book can clip a clothespin labeled with her or his name on the edge of the sign. At the beginning of independent reading each day, Mrs. Shale will confer with these students in the classroom library, studying their reading logs and highlighting potential books and strategies for choosing books successfully and independently.

During a "great books" group meeting. When several students struggle with book choice over an extended period, Mrs. Shale forms a "great books" small group. She pulls these students together once or twice a week during independent reading to reinforce book-selection lessons, recommend interesting books, and spend time with them in the classroom library. These are most often students who are not reading at grade level and haven't yet gotten hooked on books.

By encouraging her students to consider a variety of options when selecting books and expecting them to do so independently, Mrs. Shale hopes to help her students leave elementary school with the skills and know-how to continue to find great next reads.

Reflect on Chapter 5

This chapter provides some of the nitty-gritty details for helping students navigate the classroom library. Ultimately the success of their shopping trips depends on your instilling a love of reading, flooding your classroom with books, organizing your library, and helping your students find a steady stream of great next reads. Use Figure 5.8 to plan for successful book shopping in your classroom.

Figure 5.8

Chapter 5 Reflection and Plan

Steps I can take to make shopping happen regularly and efficiently for all students.

Steps I can take to make sure shopping results in joyful selection of good-fit books.

SIX

TEACH PURPOSEFUL STRATEGIES FOR FINDING GREAT BOOKS

> Providing students with the opportunity to choose their own books to read empowers and encourages them. It strengthens their self-confidence, rewards their interests, and promotes a positive attitude toward reading by valuing the reader and giving him or her a level of control.
>
> —Donalyn Miller, *The Book Whisperer:*
> *Awakening the Inner Reader in Every Child*

Help students develop book-finding skills that support success and engagement:

1. Deepen your own understanding of the choices readers make (pages 64–65).
2. Help students develop skills for finding books they *can* read (pages 65–74).
3. Help students develop skills for finding books they *want* to read (pages 74–79).

When students have good-fit books they've chosen for themselves, independent reading soon becomes a favorite time of day. They can't wait to get started and often don't want to stop. Getting the right books into their hands matters more than almost anything else in the reading classroom. Which books students encounter will ultimately determine their level of success, engagement, and joyful reading.

Get Your Students on Board

"When you discover a love of books, your world will get larger. You will go places, have adventures, see things, meet people, and learn things you never dreamed possible. Discovering a favorite author or genre or series, or a topic you want to find out more about, is the start of an amazing and unending journey. One great read will lead to another. When you study the books you are reading and think deeply about why you love them, you will learn about yourself as a reader and a person and you will get important information to help you choose your next book. If you are lucky, you will always have a lineup of next reads, maybe in your reading bucket, maybe on your nightstand, maybe just in your head, but they will be there, waiting for you like patient friends, full of promise, adventure, and information yet to be discovered and explored. My job, this year, is to help you develop that love of books and of reading."

6.1 Deepen Your Own Understanding of the Choices Readers Make

How do you harness the power of choice to help your students become successful lifelong readers? The three factors that contribute to successful text selection are shown in Figure 6.1.

Figure 6.1 Three Factors Contributing to Successful Book Selection

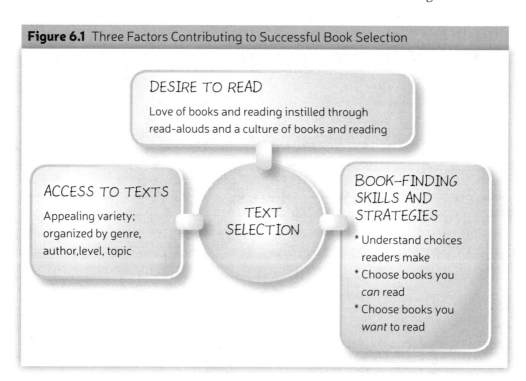

DESIRE TO READ
Love of books and reading instilled through read-alouds and a culture of books and reading

ACCESS TO TEXTS
Appealing variety; organized by genre, author, level, topic

TEXT SELECTION

BOOK-FINDING SKILLS AND STRATEGIES
* Understand choices readers make
* Choose books you *can* read
* Choose books you *want* to read

When you commit to offering students choice, you commit to teaching book-finding skills patiently and persistently. Becoming skilled book shoppers is an ongoing process. When you give your students choice, you don't say, "Now it's your job to figure out what you are going to read." Instead, you partner with them in a quest to find the books that matter most. Whether or not you consider yourself a voracious reader, you can help your students find great books by spending time honestly studying your own habits and preferences as a reader:

* **You generally don't read things you can't decipher or understand.** However, when you believe something important to you is buried in its complicated content, you are willing to push yourself through hard material.
* **You don't choose things that don't interest you.** But your interests evolve and change with time and so do the things you read.
* **People rarely tell you what you have to read.** However, you do seek and accept suggestions from other people with similar interests. You find and follow favorite authors, favorite topics, and favorite genres.
* **You don't read to earn prizes or praise.** But great reads fulfill and reward you in real ways.
* **You don't take comprehension quizzes after each book or chapter.** Yet you love to visit with others about what you have read, how it affected you, and what you liked and didn't like about it.
* **You read more than one thing at a time.** Starting, stopping, switching, and coming back to books are not uncommon. All this back-and-forth doesn't seem to compromise your reading life; if anything, it's enriched when you have more than one book going at a time.
* **When a great books ends, you sometimes aren't ready to jump right into something else.** Sometimes a story is so touching you don't want to leave it yet, even though it's over. Sometimes you immediately go back to page 1 and begin again. Other times you return to favorite parts and relish them once more.

Book-Selection Skills Develop Over Time

Beware! When you first give students more choice in what they read, something predictable will happen: they will choose books that are not good fits—books that are too difficult or too easy, books they don't understand, books they don't really care about. I say this not to scare you off but so you won't be surprised or think this is a challenge unique to your classroom or your students. All kids choose books that aren't right for them at one time or another.

 # 6.2 Help Students Develop Skills for Finding Books They *Can* Read

When young readers choose books for themselves, success rides on selecting books that are neither too easy nor too difficult. When they consistently spend time with texts that are too easy, they don't have the opportunity to stretch and grow as readers. When they spend too much time with texts that are too difficult, they are susceptible to frustration and disengagement. But spending *some* time with easier or more difficult books is something all readers do. The trick is to help kids spend most of their time with books that fit well with both their interests *and* their reading levels.

Potential Teaching Points Related to Finding Good-Fit Books

• •

- ✳ Readers understand the importance of finding good-fit books.
- ✳ Readers preview a book and decide whether it's a good fit before they make a choice.
- ✳ Readers who spend too much time with texts that are too easy don't grow as readers.
- ✳ It's important for all readers to have some challenges, but not so many that they get frustrated.
- ✳ Matching readers with books they *can* read is one part of the equation:

can read + *want* to read = *good* fit

• •

Success Levels

You need to be familiar with the concept of independent, instructional, and frustration levels to really understand what a good fit is. The extremely practical and versatile running record (Clay 2002) lets you determine how accurately a student is able to read a text at a given level. Considering the accuracy rate with which a child reads (percentage of words read correctly) helps you determine which level of texts will be a good match with the child's independent and instructional reading levels. It also reveals the kinds of errors a child is making so you can select strategic next teaching points. You can learn more about running records in Chapter 12. For a basic understanding of the relationship between accuracy rates and reading success, see Figure 6.2.

INDEPENDENT READING LEVEL

During independent reading, you want students to spend the majority of their time with texts that allow them to experience high levels of success with occasional opportunities to stretch their skills. For the most part, they should practice reading independently with texts they can read with a high rate of accuracy (95 percent or above). These books ensure success as well as provide enough challenge that there are learning opportunities. At this level of success, readers can read with enough accuracy and fluency to build the meaning of the text in their minds.

Figure 6.2 Understanding Reading Accuracy Rates

Success Level	Accuracy Level	When These Texts Work Best	Student Success Level
Independent	95%–100%	Independent reading	I can read these texts independently. They will help me develop fluency, comprehension, and confidence as a reader.
Instructional	90%–94%	Supported reading	I can read these texts with support or extra effort. They will help me stretch to learn new skills for solving problems and understanding texts.
Frustration	89% or less	Future reading (goal books)	I'm not ready for long stretches of these texts yet. Left alone with these books, I am likely to get frustrated, pretend to read, or disengage from the reading process.

INSTRUCTIONAL READING LEVEL

Students' instructional reading level tells you what types of texts are right for them when you are there to provide some level of scaffolding or strategic support (during a guided reading lesson, for example). Every successful reading teacher needs to develop skills for providing guided instruction to individuals and small groups. (You can learn more about small-group instruction in Chapter 8.)

FRUSTRATION LEVEL

Kids can't learn to read with material that is over their heads. You can't expect them to spend twenty to forty minutes a day reading material that's too hard for them. When the text is too hard, kids get frustrated, disengage, and create classroom management issues—and they certainly don't develop a love of reading.

Start Learning to Estimate Accuracy Level

Since reading less than 90 percent of the words accurately leads to frustration, apply some quick math to help you judge the fitness of a book. If a child misses more than one out of ten words, the text is probably going to be frustrating. Calculating a 10 percent error rate is easy. Count the words in a paragraph and then have the child read it. If there are seventy-two words and he makes seven errors, the reading is pretty difficult. If there are sixty-four words and the child makes only three errors, the text is possibly a good fit. There is much more to this, of course: this is a starting point, a rule of thumb to get you going. Eventually, you'll want to take a quick running record to determine readability. But you don't have to do it all at once.

A fifth-grade teacher wonders: "My kids have to be able to read at their grade level. That's the level at which their textbooks and the state tests are written. How is having a fifth grader read at a second-grade level going to help prepare him for the reality of what he will be asked to read in school?"

A possible solution: This is a valid concern. Just handing kids a lower-level text is not enough, but neither is giving them only grade-level texts they are unable to read. All kids need grade-level texts and tasks during some part of their day. But independent reading is a time for independence, success, and high volume, none of which is possible with texts that are way too difficult. Most students reading below grade level have already developed identities as unsuccessful readers. Finding readable and interesting texts for these students is an urgent priority. If reading is always difficult and frustrating, they will continue to check out as readers and as learners. But if you can help them see themselves as capable and see reading as interesting or enjoyable, you can reverse the tide. Once they have texts they can and want to read, you can elevate them skill by skill, strategy by strategy. At the same time you can share grade-level (or higher) books with them during your daily read-aloud, explicitly modeling proficient reader skills and strategies.

Use Reading Levels as Guides, Not Rigid Rules

I prefer the term *good fit* rather than *just right* especially with regard to reading level, because reading level is *not* precise; it is determined not only by the complexity of the text but also by the background knowledge, interest, and vocabulary of the reader. *Good fit* implies that there is a range of books that will work well for a reader. There is no formula for labeling students and their texts and matching them exactly. Nor is that what we want to do. On one hand, we want to be able to help students select books they can read successfully. On the other hand, we don't want to become so dependent on our letter and number leveling systems that we no longer let common sense and student individuality guide our decisions.

Many schools use a consistent system for talking and thinking about what makes books more or less difficult to read, especially during the early elementary years. Grade equivalent rankings and the Lexile framework are helpful in the intermediate grades but are much too broad for the youngest readers. Benchmark assessments for determining a child's instructional and independent reading levels, together with book collections at least partially organized using the same leveling system, make matching readers with books simpler and more efficient. Knowing a child's current reading level within a graduated scale, you are better able to match the student with books that will support both success *and* growth. Using a benchmark assessment to determine independent and instructional reading levels allows you to target instruction at the appropriate reading level as well as monitor whether students are showing steady and adequate growth over time by reading increasingly more difficult levels of texts.

Examples of Benchmarking Systems

* Fountas and Pinnell's *Benchmark Assessment System*
* *Developmental Reading Assessment, 2nd Edition Plus* (DRA2+)
* Teachers College Reading and Writing Project's Fiction Reading Level Assessments: http://readingandwritingproject.org/resources/assessments/running-records

If your school doesn't use a benchmark assessment system or your classroom library isn't leveled, don't panic. Eventually you will want both, especially if you're teaching in the primary grades. But there are still many ways to help kids find books that are a good match. Even teachers who use text-leveling systems recognize that sooner or later all children need to learn to choose books that are a good fit without the aid of labels, stickers, or colored dots. The strategies explained in the following sections help students find books at their reading level that are a good fit.

Figure 6.3 Three Ways to Read a Book Anchor Chart

Easy Ways Kids Can Find Good-Fit Books Today

There are four strategies that students can use immediately to select appropriate books: learn three ways to read a book; use an analogy; try a page or section of the book; and monitor meaning while reading.

LEARN THREE WAYS TO READ A BOOK

Teach students that every book doesn't need to be read word by word, cover to cover. This is especially true in the primary grades, when the majority of books are picture books and students' reading skills are just emerging. For emergent readers and beginning English learners, it is helpful to teach students to interact with a text in a variety of ways (Sulzby 1985):

1. **Read the pictures.** Even if your students aren't familiar with a book, there is much to "read" by studying the pictures. Be sure to model with an unfamiliar book. Fiction that includes strong, supportive pictures works well, but there is also a great deal children can observe, learn, and infer from a nonfiction text without reading a single word.

2. **Retell the story.** Once students are familiar with a story, paging through the book prompts them to retell it in language similar to that read by a more skilled reader. This is an important step to later fluent reading. A readily available basket or tub of familiar read-alouds (perhaps several copies of each) supports this type of reading.

3. **Read the words.** When kids are ready, they can read a book word by word.

See the example anchor chart in Figure 6.3.

Eventually your students need to spend the majority of their time reading words. That will come. In the beginning, making them aware that reading the pictures and retelling the story are valid ways to read independently lets you establish independent reading routines for all your students from the very first day and dramatically increases the variety of suitable texts.

Teaching Points Related to Three Ways to Read a Book

....

- ✱ Readers sometimes read the pictures.
- ✱ Readers sometimes retell a familiar story.
- ✱ Readers sometimes read the words.

....

Figure 6.4 Find a Good Fit Anchor Chart

USE AN ANALOGY

A wonderful way to introduce your students to good-fit books is through analogy. An analogy is a story that helps us remember a concept. Many teachers use the story of Goldilocks to introduce the concept of a good fit. Other teachers use a shoe analogy developed by the Sisters in *The Daily 5* (Boushey and Moser 2014). Both of these are good ways to teach kids the importance of finding books that are right for them.

I use an analogy about swimming and water depth to help kids think about finding books they *can* read: they consider both the dangers of going into water that is too deep and the boredom of spending time in water that is too shallow for them to develop their swimming skills. Both height and swimming skill determine the right water level for an individual swimmer, and the level changes with practice and lots of time spent in the water. (See Figure 6.4.) Which analogy you use doesn't matter. Just choose one you're comfortable with, bring in some props (swimming gear, shoes, porridge bowls) and start a conversation with your kids about good-fit books.

Potential Teaching Points to Create an Analogy for Finding Good-Fit Books

* Readers sometimes compare book choice to Goldilocks' choosing a bowl of porridge or a chair.
* Readers sometimes compare book choice to swimming in water that is too shallow, too deep, or just the right depth to grow as a swimmer without being in danger.

TRY A PAGE OR SECTION OF A BOOK

When students are looking for good books, they need to open a book and read a section to see how it goes. Does it feel like a good fit? Is it too easy? Too tricky? Some teachers introduce a finger-counting rule as a simple tool kids can use to judge whether or not a book is too hard for them:

1. Open the book to any page.

2. Start reading.

3. Put a finger up each time you encounter a tricky spot (a word you can't figure out, a sentence you can't understand, etc.).

4. If you put up [a quantity determined by age or reading level] fingers before reaching the end of the page, the book may not be a good fit for you; you might want to look for a different book.

5. If you get to the end of the page before you put up [quantity] fingers, the book might be a good fit for you, especially if you are interested in the topic.

See Figure 6.5.

This strategy is typically taught using five fingers, but depending on the reading level, you might use two or three fingers instead. It works best with students reading at the later-first-grade level or above, since it's difficult to apply to emergent texts that have only a few words per page and less than a hundred words in all.

Figure 6.5 Five Finger Test Anchor Chart

5 Finger Test
*Read 1 page.
*Put up 1 finger for each tricky spot.

0- It may be easy for you.
1-2- It may be a good-fit.
3-4- If you try it, go slow.
5+- Maybe save it for later.

Potential Teaching Points Related to Trying a Page or a Section of a Book

· ·

* Readers try a book out by reading a page or two.
* Readers pay attention to how many tricky spots they run into when trying out a book.
* Readers sometimes count tricky spots—the five- [three-, two-] finger rule—to find good-fit books.

· ·

MONITOR MEANING WHILE READING

As time goes on, your kids will become more comfortable with the concept of good-fit books, and you'll have more time to teach them how good readers choose books and monitor their understanding and enjoyment. Most important, you'll teach them to listen to what's going on in their heads while they're reading, monitor their understanding, and watch for signs of frustration or disengagement.

Potential Teaching Points Related to Monitoring Meaning

· ·

* Readers choose books they can mostly understand.
* Readers pay attention to how hard the work feels when they're reading.
* Readers listen to their thinking as they read and notice when they are confused or feeling lost.

· ·

Ways to Approach Difficult Books

Every teacher of reading encounters children who choose books that are too difficult. How you respond provides the child with important information. If you say, "Jackie, that book is too difficult for you. You need to choose a book you can really read," Jackie will likely leave the conversation with a reinforced idea that she is not a skilled reader and that the things she might really want as a reader are off-limits to her. Teach kids the following strategies for dealing with books they've chosen that seem too difficult.

IDENTIFYING GOAL BOOKS

When a child is obviously aching to read a book that is too difficult, you might say, "I noticed you've chosen a really challenging book. What can you tell me about why you want to read this book?" Whatever the child says next is a clue to his or her hopes and dreams as a reader and a person. For example:

* He wants to read chapter books.
* She wants to read books about wizards.

* He wants to learn more about how airplanes work.
* She wants to read what her friends are reading.

You can now reaffirm the importance of doing lots of reading at the appropriate level and commit to finding books within the child's reading range that match the genre or topic the child is interested in. In the meantime, the more difficult book can be framed as a goal book, one that they strive to be able to read soon.

Potential Teaching Points Related to Understanding Goal Books

* Readers need to read *lots* of good-fit books to build a strong and solid base for more difficult books.
* Readers need to work hard and read lots to build their reading muscles.
* Every reader starts from a different place and moves at a different pace.
* It's good to have goals and visual reminders of where we want to be someday.
* It's OK to spend a little time with books that are too challenging, but it's more important to spend most of your time reading books that are a good fit.

TAKING IT SLOWLY

Sometimes students are able to make it through challenging books because of their high interest and determination. From time to time, you'll support readers in choosing books that would typically be too challenging, because they have enough grit and enthusiasm to overcome their frustration. However, you'll need to coach them on strategies for reading slowly, in chunks, and doing lots of rereading as they go.

Potential Teaching Points Related to Reading Challenging Books

* Readers sometimes choose books they know are very challenging and commit to reading them more than once.
* Readers sometimes choose books they know are challenging and plan to read them in small chunks rather than all at once.

ABANDONING A BOOK

Although habitually abandoning books isn't productive, all readers do it from time to time. Recognizing that a book is not a good fit and making a wiser selection is an important skill. Of course, you don't want students to become "book hoppers," but when a child recognizes on his own that a book isn't a good fit, you can celebrate his ability to recognize that and move on to more productive work.

Potential Teaching Points Related to Abandoning Books

* Readers abandon books they don't understand.
* Readers abandon books that turn out to have too many difficult words.
* Readers abandon books they don't find interesting or enjoyable.
* Readers learn from their choices and try to find books they can stick with.

6.3 Help Students Develop Skills for Finding Books They *Want* to Read

Nobody ever became a passionate lifelong reader without getting connected to texts she or he couldn't put down. As a caring adult helping to cultivate book-loving kids, one of your most important roles is showering kids with possibilities about what to read. Conversations about great books   book talks, book trailers, book lists, and recommendations—are one way to do this. The following ideas may help.

Readers Make Authentic Choices

As you support your students' book choices, remember that choice is ultimately about finding a text you really care about and want to read. Contests or other extrinsic rewards should never drive book choice. You want to teach your kids to love to read for reading's sake, not to compete for the most computerized points or stars on a chart.

Potential Teaching Points Related to Finding Great Books

* Readers choose books for real reasons.
* Readers are excited when they read great books.
* Having a great book to read is what makes reading so magical.

Readers Read for a Variety of Purposes

Sometimes readers simply want to be entertained. Or they find a topic so fascinating they have to know more about it. They read about things that have a powerful connection to their own lives. If you have a purpose in mind when you start to read, you are more likely to enjoy and comprehend what you are reading. Helping young readers understand that there is a range of purposes for reading and that readers often have a specific purpose in mind when they go looking helps them make better book choices.

Potential Teaching Points Related to Reasons Readers Choose Books

- Readers choose books they will enjoy.
- Readers look for books that interest them.
- Readers look for books that teach them how to do something.
- Readers look for books that help them make a connection to something important.
- Readers sometimes want to explore or learn more about a topic.
- Readers sometimes read a favorite book (or part of a book) more than once.

Readers Are Always on the Hunt for More Great Books

Readers don't wait until they're between books to look for something new to read. Instead, they are always collecting ideas. Readers use lots of different resources to help them find great books. When it's time to go to the library, they are armed with ideas that will ensure their hunt is successful. In today's digital age, students have more access than ever to the recommendations of other young readers via lists, blogs, and videos.

Potential Teaching Points Related to Finding Ideas About What to Read

- Readers use lots of different strategies for getting ideas about what else to read.
- Readers get ideas for book choices from other people.
- Readers share book recommendations with one another.
- Readers use lists and blogs to find new ideas about what to read.
- Readers keep a list of books they might like to read in the future.

Knowing About Yourself Can Help You Find Great Books

We don't all think the same books are great. All the things we know about ourselves as people are potential clues to help us find great books. Figure 6.6 is a chart that will help students use what they know about themselves to direct their book choice. (You can adapt it to reflect your students' interests.) Sometimes, it's easier to get the feel for this by thinking about someone else's interests.

Readers Think About *Why* They Love Some Books More than Others

When kids find a book they love, it's time to have them do some deep thinking. What is it about this book? Is it the repeating pattern? The outrageous characters? The suspense? The struggles that the characters face? The diagrams and illustrations that make the learning come alive? When kids examine why they love a book, they get clues not only about themselves as readers but also about who they are as people.

Figure 6.6 Using What I Know About Myself to Choose Books

What I Know About Myself	The Type of Books I Might Be Interested In
I love baseball.	Baseball books Other sports books
My mom just had a baby.	Stories about families with new babies Stories about being an older sibling
I just moved to this school.	Stories about moving Stories about being the new kid at school Stories about wanting a friend
I have an insect collection.	Books about collecting bugs Books about the lives of insects Stories with insects as characters

Potential Teaching Points Related to Using One Great Book to Find Another

- ✖ Readers think about what it is they like and don't like about the books they read.
- ✖ Readers think about their favorite books to learn more about what they love.
- ✖ Readers ask themselves, "Why did I love this book more than some others?"
- ✖ Readers look for more books that include the things they love.

The Power of Finding Favorites

Discovering favorite authors, series, genres, or topics is a powerful way to inform choice. Use interactive read-alouds to introduce students to possibilities, and end your reading by saying, "If you loved this book, you might like to try other books by the same author [in the same series, of this type, about this topic, etc.]." Reading aloud from the first book in a series can inspire students to explore the subsequent titles.

Potential Teaching Points Related to the Power of Finding Favorites

- ✖ Readers may reread favorite books more than once.
- ✖ Readers have favorite authors and read many of their books.
- ✖ Readers have favorite topics they like to read about.
- ✖ Readers have favorite types and genres of books they like to read.

Gently Pull Students Out of Ruts

Sometimes a student falls so in love with a particular author, series, or topic that she or he doesn't read anything else. Ever. Since it's far better to have a reader obsessing over a certain type of book than floundering to find a good fit, you needn't rush to deal with this too soon. Figure 6.7 suggests some ways to steer stuck readers gently toward considering similar but slightly different options.

Figure 6.7 Ideas for Helping Stuck Readers

A student who is stuck on . . .	Might be willing to try . . .
Informational books on a particular topic (sports, sea life, horses)	Fiction that includes a strong connection to these same topics
Magic Tree House series	Magic Tree House Fact Tracker series (nonfiction linked to the topics in the series), other fantasy or adventure series
Motorcycles	Race cars, big machinery, ships, submarines, jet skis, etc.
Dinosaurs	Other interesting large animals (elephants, rhinos, whales, etc.)
Junie B. Jones	Other books about kids with spunk and spirit (Ramona, for example)
Mo Willems books	Other humorous books: Fly Guy books, by Tedd Arnold Splat the Cat books, by Robb Scotton Pete the Cat books, by James Dean Bad Kitty books, by Nick Bruel

Expose Kids to New Titles, Topics, or Genres

A great way to expose children to a lot of books in a short amount of time or help them get to know more about a particular basket in (or new additions to) the classroom library is to conduct a book pass with either a small group of children with similar reading levels or the whole class. The following box outlines the procedure for conducting a book pass.

Hook Kids Through Book Trailers and Author or Illustrator Videos

You love getting the inside scoop, don't you? Well, that's what a book trailer or author or illustrator video can do for your kids. In a world where it sometimes seems books don't stand a chance against competition from movies, television, tablets, and video games, the video trailer meets

How to Conduct a Book Pass

1. Select the same number of books as you have children.

2. Seat the children in a circle or other formation that makes it easy to pass a book to the next person without getting out of their seats.

3. Randomly give one book to each student.

4. Set the timer for a designated period (two minutes is usually enough).

5. During each period, children examine the book, read the back cover or inside jacket, read snippets of the book, or look at the pictures.

6. When the timer goes off, students decide whether they want to keep the book and spend more time with it or pass it on to the next person. (Students can keep any book for as many successive periods as they like.)

7. Continue in this way for a number of timed periods.

Have students record titles they are interested in on their lists of possible future reads (see Appendix D, available at www.heinemann.com/products/E06155.aspx). They can keep one book to start reading immediately if they wish. Not everyone will get a new book or an idea for a future read every time, but many students will.

them on their turf, capturing their curiosity and leaving them hungry to have the book in their hands. Another beautiful thing about trailers is that they often tell the story behind the story. Knowing how a book, its story, or the illustrations came to be helps children view the reading experience through a different lens.

Video book trailers can be magic, especially for teachers who are intimidated at the thought of recommending books that truly excite kids. Consider the following when choosing video book trailers to use in the classroom:

1. **Always start with an amazing book.** Start with award winners, highly rated books, books from favorite lists, and so on. The best book trailer won't matter a lick if the book is a dud.

2. **Consider books written by favorite authors or books in a series.** The power of a book trailer is multiplied if it can hook a reader into a natural progression of books.

3. **Take the time to search for a truly great trailer.** Don't show a boring video. Publisher, bookseller, and author and illustrator websites usually contain the best trailers.

4. **Always preview a trailer before sharing it with your kids.** Don't share the first video you find on YouTube.

5. **Add your two cents.** Don't just show. Tell your kids why you think this book is trailer worthy. Set the stage.

6. **Have at least one copy of the book in your hand when you show the trailer.** The idea of a trailer is to make kids hungry to read the book. Be ready to feed the hunger.

7. **Post favorite trailers on the class blog or website for future reference.** This will become a resource for students who might not be ready for this book now but want to consider it in the future.

Harness the Power of the Internet

No matter what book dilemma you are trying to solve in your classroom, no matter how little you currently know about the best titles for the age group you work with, no matter how puzzling it might be to find series, topics, and authors at the right readability levels for your kids, a quick search on the Internet will steer you in the right direction. Try search terms like these:

1. best books for fourth-grade boys

2. books for kids who love firefighters

3. fantasy series for the intermediate grades

4. realistic fiction about courageous girls

5. I've read every Judy Moody book, what next?

Also check out online book lists; lists of award winners; children's literature book reviews and blogs; and the Caldecott, Newberry, Horn Book, and IndieBound websites.

Reflect on Chapter 6

Nobody can tell you how many lessons your students will need on book selection. It depends on how much experience they have already had with book selection, how your book collection is organized, what books it contains, who your students are, and how quickly they grasp these concepts.

As you begin, your students will most likely need many lessons on book choice. Don't rush it, and don't be surprised to find it's more difficult for them than you imagined. Also, keep in mind that because kids' needs and interests are constantly changing, they may benefit from revisiting lessons you taught previously.

Respond to the questions in Figure 6.8, then use those reflections to list three to five manageable action steps you can commit to *starting today* to increase student skill and success with book selection (see Figure 6.9).

Figure 6.8 Reflection on Three Factors Related to Successful Book Selection

Reflection Questions	Responses and Next Steps
Desire to Read (Chapter 1) Am I nurturing a true love of reading in my classroom? Do I surround students with books to inspire them as readers? Do I read aloud with passion and commitment every day?	
Available Text (Chapter 5) Have I made sure that my classroom has a well-stocked, appealing, and accessible collection of books? **Book-Shopping Routines** (Chapter 5) Do I have a well-developed system to ensure all children can regularly access the classroom library to shop for books?	
Book-Finding Skills (Chapter 6) Have I taught students strategies for finding books they can read? Have I taught students strategies for finding books they want to read? Have I created a true reading community, in which talk about great books abounds? Have I taught strategies for using one great book to find another?	

Figure 6.9 Chapter 6 Action Steps and Timeline

What I Commit to Do/Teach	Realistic Time Line

SEVEN

DELIVER CLEAN, FOCUSED WHOLE-GROUP INSTRUCTION

Teaching children to read and providing them with something worthwhile to read is not a job for the faint of heart in this world. But I'll keep at it, and I won't be alone. You'll come too.

We're fortunate, you know. Too many people in this world spend their lives doing work that doesn't really matter in the great scheme of things, but bringing children and books together does matter. And we get to do it.

—Katherine Paterson, "Back from IBBY"

To develop strong, independent readers:

1. Use a minilesson format for whole group instruction (pages 81–86).
2. Gather your class for a few minutes of strategic reflection at the end of each day's independent reading (pages 86–89).

7.1 Use a Minilesson Format to Structure Whole-Group Instruction

Teachers working toward high levels of success with independent reading often support the journey with a whole-group instructional tool called a *minilesson*. Minilessons are a simple way to feed your kids, bit by bit, through modeling and shared practice, a steady diet of insider secrets about what successful readers do. Each day, you teach just one thing. If you were to explain minilessons to your kids, it might sound something like this:

> "Readers, every day just before independent reading, we'll meet in
> the gathering area and I'll teach you something that can help you
> become a better reader."

That's it. It just takes a commitment to teach one thing each day and teach it well.

As the name implies, minilessons are intentionally quite short—ten or fifteen minutes at most. And they *can* be short, because they focus on one clear, explicit teaching point. One. Clear. Explicit. You choose the teaching point based on what you know your kids can already do and what you believe they are ready to do next.

Remember those bread crumbs I've been dropping along the trail, all the strategies you might teach your readers? Every one of them is a potential teaching point for a whole-group minilesson. Later, if some kids still need more help, you can follow up with flexible small-group instruction focused on these same points.

Minilesson Structure: Connect, Teach, Engage, Link

The steps in delivering a high-quality minilesson have been well defined by Lucy Calkins (2001). They gradually release responsibility to the student, while keeping your teaching clean, consistent, and focused. The steps happen in the same sequence during every minilesson:

1. **Connect.** Begin each minilesson by making some sort of a connection. This section of the lesson is very brief, many times only a minute. You activate prior knowledge or learning by telling the students how today's learning connects to something they already know about through past experience.

Connect

* Get students interested by creating a connection to the content of the lesson.
* Connect today's learning to a past experience and/or prior knowledge.
* Connect today's learning to the previous lesson.
* Connect today's learning with their ongoing efforts to become better readers.

Example Language

Yesterday we learned . . .

We've been thinking a lot about . . .

Have you ever noticed that sometimes when you're reading . . . ?

I've been listening to your conversations about . . . and thinking that it might
   be helpful to . . .

Remember yesterday I showed you how to . . .

I've been watching you and I noticed that some of you . . .

Have any of you noticed how difficult it can be to . . . ?

2. Teach. Tell students what you will teach them and then teach it, using explicit modeling and sharing your thinking. This is where you take the most ownership, or responsibility, for the task and the students take the least. The students are free of all cognitive demands except watching and listening.

Teach

- ✳ Tell students exactly what you are going to teach them.
- ✳ Tell them why it matters or is useful.
- ✳ Teach it explicitly by modeling, using an analogy, and/or thinking aloud.

Example Language

There's one thing I want to teach you today.

Today, I have one tip for you.

Today, I want to let you in on a secret that some readers use.

Today, I want to show you what I do when . . .

Watch as I show you how to . . .

Did you notice how I . . . ?

Watch closely while I show this again . . .

When this happens, I think to myself . . . and then I . . .

3. Engage. Sometimes referred to as active involvement, this is the stage where we begin to release some responsibility for the task by having students try it out. You might have the students do the task with you, try it with their partners, or watch while a student models for the class and you narrate. You'll get a sense of how well students understand and are able to perform the task.

Engage

- ✳ Start to release responsibility to the students through guided practice.
- ✳ Students practice with you, while you watch, or with partners. They may also observe while other students demonstrate and you narrate.

Example Language

Let's try this together.

Try this with a partner.

Watch while [child's name] shows us how this would look.

I'm going to do this first, and then I want you to try it in the same way.

Take a book out of your book box and try this for yourself while I watch and listen.

4. Link. Prepare students to apply this teaching to their work as readers, today and in the future.

Link

* Prepare students to transfer the learning to their own reading.
* Restate the teaching point.
* Remind them why it will be useful today and in the future.

Example Language

Today and every day, when you read independently . . .

Today and every day, when you are selecting books to read . . .

Today and every day, when you get confused about what you're reading . . .

Today and every day, think about . . . as you read.

When you're reading today, maybe you'll decide to try . . .

Anchor the Learning with a Chart

Remember the anchor charts described in Chapter 2? You can build them with your students during a minilesson. This may happen during the teaching phase (you explicitly state some truth about reading and write it on a chart) or the engagement phase (you and your students cocreate an element of a chart). You may also refer or add something to a chart created in a past lesson. See Figure 7.1 for an example anchor chart.

Figure 7.1 Figure Out Word Meaning Anchor Chart

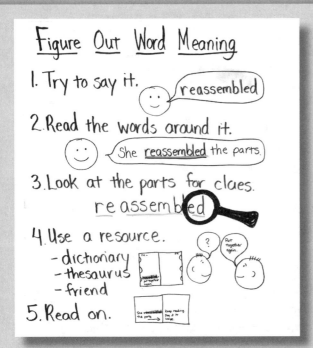

Teach Your Readers, Not a Text

Although you'll usually use a text to demonstrate the point you're making, the minilesson is not about teaching the content of a specific text. You're teaching a *strategy* or *skill* that successful readers use. For example, you might use Catherine D. Hughes' *First Big Book of Dinosaurs* to demonstrate a feature of nonfiction or a fix-up strategy, but your purpose is to teach the strategy—readers use a table of contents to find what they are looking for in a nonfiction book; readers use fix-up strategies when they get confused—not to teach about dinosaurs.

Step Inside a Classroom

A Minilesson About Staying in Your Spot to Get Lots of Reading Done

Connect: "Readers, yesterday we learned that readers choose a spot for reading that is comfortable and free of distractions so that they are able to focus on their reading. Today, I want to teach you that real readers stay in that spot the whole time, getting as much reading done as possible. They don't get up or walk around the room; they stay put the whole time, reading and thinking about their book. This is easy for them, because they have books that they love and care about, so they don't want to waste time doing other things."

Teach: "Watch me as I show what staying in one place and focusing on reading my books looks like. Since I've chosen a comfortable spot, I'm not feeling wiggly and uncomfortable. Since I have great books to read, I'm excited to get started. As I'm reading, if I get the urge to get up and move around the room, I look at the anchor chart and remind myself to stay in my spot. Sometimes when I'm feeling restless, it's because I'm not that interested in the book I've chosen; in that case, I can choose a different book from my box."

Engage: "I'm wondering, can one of you help me demonstrate how it looks when you are up and out of your spot during independent reading?" Carmen raises her hand. "Carmen, will you demonstrate what it might look like if you were not staying in your spot?"

Carmen says, "You mean I leave my spot and walk around or something?"

Yes. Remind us of some things that could happen that don't really look like focused reading."

Carmen sits down on the floor and acts like she is reading for a moment and then says, "Well, I might walk over and talk to one of my friends."

"Yes, show me what that would look like." Carmen walks across to a friend and whispers in her ear. "What else?"

"I might go to the library and look for different books."

"Okay. Show us." Carmen goes to the library. "Turn and talk to your partner about the choices Carmen is making, and what she could do instead." The teacher listens in and identifies a few students she will ask to repeat their comments when the class reconvenes.

"Now, Carmen, before you go will you show us what staying in your spot looks like? Watch carefully as Carmen demonstrates staying in her spot and connected with her books the whole time, so that you can turn and talk with your partner about all the things she is doing right this time." After Carmen demonstrates, students talk with their partners about the characteristics of her engagement.

Link: "Readers, today when you get to your reading spots, practice staying in your spots the whole time so you can get as much reading done as possible. That's what successful readers do."

Organize Lessons into Units of Study

Ultimately, you'll want to organize your lessons into bigger packages, called units of study. A unit of study is just that: a sequence of instruction in which you investigate some facet of reading—responding to characterization, making inferences, choosing good-fit books—in more depth. Each day's minilesson supports one piece of the overall unit.

The first unit of the year is often called a *launch*. Launch minilessons deal with routines and procedures for reading independently, choosing books, and becoming a person who values having a reading life. For instance, the first day you teach that readers read because they are interested in their books; the second day you teach that readers take time and care in choosing books to read; the third day you teach that readers pick reading spots that are comfortable and free of distractions; the next day you teach that readers stay in their spots the whole time they are reading.

Appendix C (available online at www.heinemann.com/products/E06155.aspx) lists potential topics for minilessons to support independent reading. They may not be the precise lessons your students will need, since I don't know your kids. But the list will get you thinking, which is what I promised to do.

Begin, and Grow as You Go

When you combine the four steps of the minilesson with your teacher instincts and the things you know about your students, you'll be on your way. Each day, choose one more thing that real readers do and teach it in a minilesson. Later, when you've fallen in love with independent reading, you may want to spend more time exploring the art of the minilesson. For now, dare to get your feet wet. Your first minilessons may feel bumpy or disconnected. You may be unsure what to teach. But stick with it. Keep reflecting and refining as you go. When you're ready, you can dig deeper, peeling back more layers of this rich and exciting work.

7.2 Gather Your Class for a Few Minutes of Strategic Reflection

You've sent your students off from a successful minilesson to read, read, read, and independent reading is now coming to a close. The time has flown by too quickly. But before you rush on to math or music or lunch, gather your students close and take a few minutes to reflect, celebrate, and look toward tomorrow.

Whatever you call it—sharing, checking in, wrapping up, providing closure—and whether you use the time to review, conduct a formative assessment, set goals, celebrate, or plan, your purpose is to reflect and look forward. It is a chance for you and your students to think deeply about how things are going, commit to continue what's working, and recognize what adjustments need to be made in the coming days.

Daily reflection, done right, is so much more than it might appear at first glance. On the surface it may look as if you're just wrapping up one activity before moving on to the next. But you are really

* modeling how reflection looks, sounds, and feels
* bolstering students' self-confidence by showcasing their smart work as readers
* assessing students' application of skills and strategies
* demonstrating your consistent commitment to high expectations for your readers
* helping students build their self-awareness of what's working and not working
* strengthening your community of readers by recognizing and celebrating one another's successes
* expanding students' capacity for self-directed learning
* providing opportunities to solve problems by working together.

Here are the essentials for daily reflection:

1. Bring your students together in the gathering area.

2. Recognize some of the successes you observed during independent reading. Later you'll push kids to stretch higher, but starting by recognizing the positive is powerful.

3. Extend the learning you've already begun by asking students to reflect on how things went today, how they want things to go in the future, and what steps will get them there. Be sure to use strong, open-ended questions to encourage deep thinking.

4. Keep it short (three to five minutes)! You certainly don't want to rob your kids of valuable reading time with drawn-out analysis. Short and sweet, but daily.

Keys to Successful Whole-Group Reflection

* Rely on partner conversations more than whole-group sharing.
* Resist the urge to skip reflection.
* Decide how to use the time you and your students spend reflecting.
* Maintain a tone of wonder and interest.

Rely on Partner Conversations More than Whole-Group Sharing

Having every child share takes too long, and your students will quickly tire of waiting through twenty-some responses for their turns. On the other hand, you don't want a few eager beavers doing all the thinking for the group. You want everyone to think about how it's going. Partner conversations allow every student to account for her or his own thinking and reflection in the same time it would take two students to share with the entire class. (For more information about using partner conversations, see Chapter 10.)

Resist the Urge to Skip Reflection

You will inevitably be tempted to skip reflection, but please reconsider. I know your schedule is tight, every minute is valuable, and the head cook will be on your case if you're late getting your kids to the lunchroom one more time. But reflection is the glue that holds learning together; if you skip it, you risk things becoming disconnected and the day's teaching point being less powerful than it could have been. The time you spend reflecting with your students at the end of their independent reading is a short but powerful way to strengthen reading skills, rituals, and routines. It is an essential ingredient in the recipe for developing self-directed learners.

Decide How to Use the Time You and Your Students Spend Reflecting

There is no right or wrong thing to focus on. The important thing is to strategically reinforce, build on, stretch, or connect your students' learning. When you do, it is more likely that the learning will impact them not just today but in the future. Figure 7.2 provides some examples of how you might use your moments of reflection.

Figure 7.2 Ideas to Support Meaningful Reflection

Purpose	What You Might Say
Link back to the day's teaching point.	Today we explored one of my favorite reasons for reading: readers read for joy! I asked you to bring an example of something you read today that gave you true joy. Now take a few minutes to share your joyful reading experience with a partner.
Review a concept learned earlier.	Readers, last week we learned that sometimes readers collect interesting words to study and consider using in their thinking, speaking, and writing. I'm excited to hear some of the interesting words you collected during your reading today. You should all have a sticky note with an interesting word which you can share with your partner now.
Reinforce a concept or routine by referring to an anchor chart.	Let's take another look at the chart showing the steps for returning books to our classroom library. I want to make sure we all understand how this can help us be good book stewards.
Highlight a student's success by giving a public compliment.	I want to share the smart work I saw Margo doing while she was reading today. When she noticed she was confused about what was happening, she backed up and reread the previous page. This really helped her, because she'd gotten distracted and missed some important details. Hearing her inner voice saying "Huh? What's happening?" helped her know she needed to back up and reread.

continues

Figure 7.2 Ideas to Support Meaningful Reflection, *cont.*

Purpose	What You Might Say
Compliment the whole group.	Readers, I just have to tell you how exciting it was to see how quickly and efficiently you all got to your reading today. What do you think are some of the factors that contributed to that success? Turn and talk with your partner.
Ask students to share a summary or segment of what they've read with a partner.	As we continue to think about the ways visualization helps a reader, I want you to describe to your partner what he or she would see when visiting the setting of the story you're reading right now.
Wonder aloud how to solve a problem.	As I've been listening during independent reading, I've been wondering about the noise level in our classroom. Let's take some time together to think about whether we're being quiet enough to concentrate on our reading or if this is something we need to work on.
Make an observation about something that didn't go so well.	Today I was a bit surprised and disappointed. Every time I started a conference, someone was tapping on my shoulder, asking me for help, rather than trying to solve his or her problems independently or with a classmate. Because of these interruptions, I got to confer with only three of the five students I'd planned to meet with today. I'm hoping we can do some problem solving about this so I won't miss out on important conferences again tomorrow.
Ask students to record on a sticky note or in their reading notebook one thing they did well and one area in which they need to stretch.	Today I want us to reflect on all the agreements on our anchor chart. Read through them, and make a note about one thing you can celebrate doing well. Now, make a note about the one thing that is most important for you to work on. Put this sticky note on the cover of your book where you'll see it right away when you start reading tomorrow.

Maintain a Tone of Wonder and Interest

When things aren't going well, students are often the first to identify it. They can be much harder on themselves than you ever would be. When you trust students to reflect honestly and suggest solutions, they may surprise you with their perceptive thinking.

Reflect on Chapter 7

Lucy Calkins often ends a minilesson by saying, "Off you go." These simple words release students to the important work of reading, applying what they've learned along the way. The template in Appendix C (available online at www.heinemann.com/products/E06155.aspx) will help you apply what you've learned here by preparing a simple minilesson and reflection for your students. Use ideas suggested in this and other chapters (and in Appendix C) to help you select a teaching point if you need help getting started. Jot some notes about what you will do in each part of the lesson. Implement the lesson, gather your kids for a share, and then use the form in Figure 7.3 to reflect on how it went. OK—off you go.

Figure 7.3 Chapter 7 Reflection on Whole Group Instruction

Reflection on Whole Group Instruction

	Yes/No	Reflection
I **gathered my students** close.		
I identified a **single teaching point** for the lesson (Appendix C can help).		
I made a clear **connection** to past learning or experience.		
I used **explicit instruction**, modeling, and/or thinking aloud to make the learning clear.		
I actively **engaged** my students during the lesson.		
I **linked** the skill or strategy back to independent reading.		
I kept the lesson **short** (15 minutes or less).		
I gathered my students for a meaningful **reflection** or share time at the end of their independent reading.		

EIGHT

PROVIDE SMART, PURPOSEFUL SMALL-GROUP INSTRUCTION

> I wanted to get better at differentiated instruction. I knew that to do this I needed to group children more flexibly and purposefully and to develop a repertoire of ways to meet their needs. I needed to find structures and methods that got at the heart of engaged, independent reading.
>
> —Jennifer Serravallo, *Teaching Reading in Small Groups: Differentiated Instruction for Building Strategic, Independent Readers*

Meet the needs of all of your learners by delivering sensible small-group instruction.

1. Make small-group work an extension of what you're already teaching, not something separate (pages 92–93).

2. Keep groups small and the time frame short (page 93).

3. Create flexible and fluid groups by daring to think beyond levels (pages 94–95).

4. Stick to one powerful teaching point that can transfer to independent reading (pages 95–97).

5. Spend most of the time listening to students read (page 97).

6. Engage the rest of the students in authentic tasks (pages 97–99).

Because students have diverse backgrounds, strengths, needs, learning styles, interests, and attention spans, even the most well-planned whole-group instruction is rarely right for everyone. Differentiation is crucial. Some kids need more explicit instruction. Some kids need more guided practice. Some kids need more support for moving from practice to application. Some kids aren't ready at the time the whole-group instruction takes place. Some kids already know what's being taught and need to be challenged to grow in other ways.

When several students have a need for additional support or a challenge in common, small-group instruction is a powerful and efficient tool. Relax! Small-group work doesn't have to be painful or unmanageable. Yes, it takes effort. But working with small groups doesn't mean seeing every student in a small group every day. There is a smarter and simpler way.

8.1 Make Small-Group Work an Extension of What You're Already Teaching, Not Something Separate

For small-group work to be simple, sensible, and manageable, you cannot think of it as one more thing you do in the reading classroom. Instead, it must extend instruction you have already presented to the whole class in a read-aloud or minilesson. The real power of whole-group instruction lies in its being used in combination with small-group instruction and one-to-one conferences. The differentiation provided in a smaller group is a bridge linking whole-group instruction to independent application (Serravallo 2010).

To create this bridge of differentiation, you need to ask yourself some important planning questions based on your whole-group instruction:

1. Who has taken on the target learning? Who has not?

2. Who could benefit from more support? More challenge?

3. What type of additional support or challenge do they need?

Step Inside a Classroom

Connecting to Your Partner's Ideas in Conversation

Previous teaching point: During an interactive read-aloud, Ms. Perez focused on helping her third graders connect their own thinking to their partners' comments in a turn-and-talk conversation. The class cocreated an anchor chart, adding new sentence frames as they were introduced:

I agree and . . .
I disagree because . . .
Tell me more about . . .

---

continues

Observation: Listening to partner conversations, Ms. Perez notices that the majority of her students are consistently making connections to their partners' comments. However, she has noticed four students who continue to pile on completely disconnected comments. For instance, after her prompt "Take a moment to think about what big idea you think the author, Robert Munsch, wanted us to be thinking about after reading *Paper Bag Princess*. Why would an author write a book like this anyway? Remember to connect your thinking to your partner's," Jack and Toby had this exchange:

> **JACK:** I think maybe the big idea is that you should be more thankful when people do nice things for you.
> **TOBY:** I thought it was sort of weird that she had to wear a paper bag the whole time.
> **JACK:** When I was, like, four I had dragons everywhere in my room, even a dragon lamp.
> **TOBY:** Well the best thing about being a dragon is you get to have fire come right out of your mouth.

Extending the learning with a small group: Later in the morning, Ms. Perez gathers the four students who need more support building their skills for connected conversation. She brings with her the anchor chart she has been using during the read-aloud. During the lesson she models a conversation with a student partner, then has the students practice in pairs. She listens in on each partnership, reinforcing success and directing them to the sentence frames on the anchor chart when needed.

8.2 Keep the Group Size Small and the Time Frame Short

This may seem obvious, but one of the key defining features of small-group instruction is the number of students in the group. You'll want to limit your groups to six or fewer students. Smaller groups mean more personal attention for each student.

You'll also want to keep your small-group lesson short—no more than fifteen minutes. This allows you to work with more groups and individuals, but more importantly, it allows your readers to get back to independent reading as soon as possible. To keep yourself accountable, set a timer at the beginning of each group lesson and when the time is up, bring the instruction to a close. Clean and short is always the goal.

8.3 Create Flexible and Fluid Groups

Flexible grouping allows you to bring various groups of students together for various reasons. Fluid means students should change groups frequently. Some groups are based on reading level; you'll form others because you've observed a common need—working on fluency, book-finding skills, or comprehension, for example. If you identify a common need and *then* form the group, you'll have not only a clear teaching objective but also a clearer means of deciding when students no longer need to be part of the group.

Some students progress more quickly than others, needing only one or two lessons on the focus strategy. That's great. Let them go. As group size shrinks, you will be able to give even more attention to those who remain. Sometimes students join the group a few lessons in. Sometimes you'll disband the group because everyone is now applying the target strategy. Some groups may exist for only one lesson. Others may meet every other day for a few weeks. Still others may meet daily for an extended period. Keep it fluid. Keep it flexible.

Step Inside a Classroom

Finding Books You Truly Care About

Previous teaching point: During whole-group minilessons, Mr. Connell has taught his third graders a number of strategies readers can use to select good-fit books.

Observation: Based on his observations and the reading logs he has been reviewing, he identifies five students who frequently choose and then abandon a book.

Extending the learning with a small group: Mr. Connell decides to meet with these students twice a week until they are able to choose appropriate books more consistently. The group meets in the classroom library, where he can demonstrate book-finding strategies and showcase potentially interesting books or genres. Each time the group meets, he reviews the students' reading logs and listens to them read aloud and retell a section of the book they're currently reading. If students have abandoned a book since the previous meeting, they come prepared to talk about what they think was wrong with that choice.

During the first meeting Isaiah says, "I don't think I'm really that good at choosing books, because I never really had to do it last year. At my other school we mostly read books the teacher gave us, and the other books we read, we didn't really have to talk about or anything."

continues

At the end of the second meeting, Josh comments on the power of reading the backs of books: "I don't know why, but I never really did that before. Now, I see it's sort of like a little book talk right there. Also, I've learned that if the back is hard to read or understand, the book probably will be too."

Keeping it fluid: Josh leaves the group after the second meeting, because he has responded immediately to the first two refresher lessons on book choice. After four meetings, Mr. Connell determines, based on their book logs and conversations, that two other students are ready to choose books independently. Isaiah, who is completely new to self-selected independent reading, and one other student are making progress but require ongoing support with this skill. Mr. Connell decides to meet with these two students twice a week, once together and once individually. During these meetings he checks on book choices and reinforces the strategies they've learned.

8.4 Stick to One Powerful Teaching Point That Can Transfer to Independent Reading

All students benefit from small-group instruction at some point. Although some teachers feel every student should work with a small group every day, I worry about pulling a student into a group without a well-identified teaching point in mind. Your students have many needs. But when planning a small-group lesson, apply the same rules you would to a minilesson or a one-to-one conference: choose one powerful teaching point. Not three. Not six. One.

Once you've chosen your teaching point, ask yourself these three questions:

* Will this help these students increase their indepedence?
* Is this an extension of something I've already taught the whole group?
* Is this within their reach?

If you can answer yes to all three questions, you've likely selected a powerful and appropriate teaching point for your small group. Gather the students and teach!

The most effective small-group work focuses on the same strategy over several days. You don't need a new and unique teaching point every day. Any time we want students to apply and integrate a strategy, it's wise to provide more than a single lesson before moving on to something new.

A strategy that helps you stay focused on a single teaching point for a small group is *first* identifying the single teachable strategy your readers need more support with and *then* deciding which text will best support your purpose. Planning in this order, you'll avoid the pitfalls of teaching *the book* rather than *the readers* in front of you.

A third-grade teacher wonders: "What are strategies, anyway?"

A possible answer: A strategy is a purposeful action that a reader can perform to help himself or herself out while reading. For example:

* Slow down.

* Reread.

* Study the pictures for clues.

* Look for chunks you know inside bigger words.

* Think about the character's actions.

* Visualize the scene in your head.

* Make an inference about what is not stated directly in the text.

Step Inside a Classroom

Checking Word Choices in More than One Way

Previous teaching point: During both shared reading and whole-group minilessons, Ms. Lopez has been helping her first-grade readers use a balanced cueing system, teaching them that readers check their word choices in more than one way.

Observation: Ms. Lopez notices several students who continue to attempt to solve a word by paying attention to its visual features but failing to consider whether the word they choose makes sense or sounds right in the sentence.

Extending the learning with a small group: Ms. Lopez starts by saying, "I'd like to invite Rosa, Amador, Felix, and Sandra to the table with me." These students respond to her invitational tone and come to the table eagerly and quickly. Ms. Lopez immediately tells them why they've gathered. "I've brought you together today to think about how readers check their word choices in more than one way. One thing I've noticed is that all of you are really good at looking closely at words for clues about how they might sound." Rosa

continues

smiles happily at the compliment. "Can you tell me about some of the things to do when you're trying to figure out a word?"

"I look for chunks," Rosa offers.

"I think about the sounds at the beginning and the end," Felix says.

"Those are both great examples of ways readers can look very closely at a word for clues. I want you to keep doing those things. They're important. But today, I want to help you remember another important way to check our word choices after we've used all we know to look closely at word parts. I want to remind you to make sure your choices make sense."

8.5 Spend Most of the Time Listening to Students Read

A text—a book, a poem, an essay, a magazine article—should be at the center of all small-group work. Whatever strategy you are teaching, you will want to quickly link it to real reading. Most of the time, students should be *reading* something in order to practice the strategy being highlighted. Either provide a copy of the same text to all the students or have them use the texts they are reading independently. As Fountas and Pinnell remind us, it's all about helping students "use and develop strategies on the run" (1996, 2).

Instead of reading round-robin style, students in small groups should read their own texts at their own rate. While they read, you'll move from student to student, listening in, assessing the needs of each individual, and providing targeted support. Remember the timer you're going to have at the table with you? It's a good idea to set it twice, to be sure you take only the first four or five minutes to explain and model the strategy and leave plenty of time for students to practice reading with you close at hand. If you run out of time before you've worked with every student, make a note to either follow up with a conference or to start with the missed students the next time you work with the group.

8.6 Engage the Rest of the Students in Authentic Tasks

For meaningful small-group work to take place, your other students need to be purposefully engaged in authentic independent literacy tasks. Not filling out worksheets or moving through time-killing workstations, but reading books, writing about books, and talking about books. When kids are reading and writing about reading every day, they won't be asking for help with instructions, plugged glue bottles, or missing game pieces. They'll have a familiar and engaging daily routine.

It takes time and attention to establish the routines that allow you to step away for fifteen minutes at a time without interruption; most teachers spend three or four weeks doing so before diving into small-group work. You may also want to establish a special signal to remind students not to interrupt you (except for blood, vomit, or fire!) when you're with a small group—perhaps a special hat, a specific-color bracelet or scarf, or a "Do Not Disturb" sign. (Come on, you'd look great in a brightly colored fedora!)

Figure 8.1 highlights common mistakes teachers make when trying to design manageable, flexible, and responsive small-group instruction and how to avoid them.

Figure 8.1 Designing Successful Small-Group Instruction

What to Avoid	What to Do Instead
Becoming overly focused on seeing every student every day	**Remember that every student doesn't need small-group instruction every day.** Fewer, more effective small groups a day are preferable to five or six. Some groups can meet every other day. Some may need to meet only once or twice a week.
Trying to see too many students at one time	**Keep groups small.** Never form a group of more than six students, and keep them smaller whenever possible. If you have more than six students with a similar need, form two groups. If ten or more students need the same instruction, you should probably present it to the whole class.
Assigning students to leveled groups and making changes only two or three times a year	**Create truly flexible groups.** Change group focus and membership as the needs of individual students change. Students who start out at the same level rarely progress at the same level. Moving in and out of groups is common.
Referring to small groups by special names (fluency group, jaguars, orange group)	**Don't name your groups.** This stops kids from analyzing the code behind the names and makes it easier to keep groups flexible. Gather students by calling their names: "I'd like to meet with Annika, Boden, Macy, and Ridge." You can then reconfigure groups without having to say things like, "I know you've been coming with the red group, but now I'd like you to come when I call the blue group."
Giving in to the temptation to try to teach many things in one lesson	**Choose one teaching point.** Small-group instruction, like whole-group minilessons, should focus on one clear, clean learning objective. Your students have many needs, but you'll be ahead of the game if you address one thing at a time and help them master it.

continues

Figure 8.1 *cont.*

What to Avoid	What to Do Instead
Grouping students only by reading level	**Group students who need to work on the same strategy.** If students at a variety of reading levels are working on the same strategy, have them practice using the texts they've selected for independent reading.
Believing you need a guide or scope-and-sequence outline for what to teach	**Teach responsively.** Small-group instruction is not the time to introduce new content. It is a tool for filling in gaps and helping students catch up by presenting familiar content in new ways. Kids are in the group because they need instruction in addition to or different from what they received when part of the whole group. No guide or script can tell you exactly what more they need or how to respond.
Spending too much time talking or telling students about a text and too little time supporting students as they read	**Ensure that students spend most of the time reading.** Reading is the most important activity whether students are receiving small-group instruction or reading independently. The difference is you are there to scaffold them in the small group, coaching as they need it.
Becoming overly focused on teaching the text	**Teach your readers, not the text.** Although your instruction may be centered on a text, you are teaching a strategy that applies to any text. Think, "How can I use this book to teach the strategy these readers need?"
Using small groups for round-robin reading	**Have all students read their own texts at their own rates.** Younger students should definitely read aloud, in a soft voice. Older students can read silently until it is their turn for you to dip in, listen, and coach them. Round-robin reading isn't effective. Let it go.
Worrying you won't know what to teach	**Trust yourself and keep it simple.** Focus on extending or strengthening something you've already taught to the whole group. Small-group differentiation doesn't mean different content; it means differences in time and approach.
Thinking students need to finish the text every time	**Teach strategies, not books.** Sometimes, especially in the intermediate grades, students will read only a small portion of a text as part of their small-group instruction. They may finish it on their own or not at all. That's OK. The important thing is understanding and applying a strategy to any book, not just this book.

Reflect on Chapter 8

Compare the six principles for small-group instruction with the way you currently work with small groups (see Figure 8.2). Where can you adjust your current practice to make your small groups more fluid, flexible, and meaningful?

Figure 8.2 Chapter 8 Plan for Applying Small Group Principles

Principles	Ways I Could Adjust My Current Practice
Keep groups small and the time frame short.	
Make small-group work an extension of what's already being taught, not something separate.	
Create truly flexible groups by daring to think beyond levels.	
Stick to one powerful teaching point that can transfer to independent reading.	
Spend most of the time listening to students read.	
Engage the rest of the students in authentic tasks.	

NINE

LEVERAGE THE POWER OF CONFERRING

Get to Know and Support Your Readers

> Just as each book, well read, makes children better readers, each conference, well taught, makes us better teachers. Our children deserve our bravest selves.
>
> —Lucy Calkins, *The Art of Teaching Reading*

Take independent reading to the next level by providing support, encouragement, and differentiation through one-to-one conferences:

1. Recognize and commit to the power of one-to-one conferences (pages 102–104).
2. Set an inviting and respectful tone for conferring (pages 104–105).
3. Follow a predictable format (pages 105–110).
4. Create a conferring routine that works for you (pages 111–116).

Imagine yourself accountable for teaching only one student this year. Not thirty-two. Not twenty-four. Not eighteen. Just one! Sound appealing? Or does it make you laugh out loud? As crazy as having just one student sounds, that's what happens during an effective reading conference. For these moments, you are not the teacher of dozens of students, and this one child is not part of a crowded classroom. It's just the two of you. No one else.

Get Your Students on Board

"As your reading teacher this year, it's my job to be a detective, learning all I can about you as a reader. One way I will get to know you better is through the reading conference.

"A conference is a special conversation between you and me—student and teacher—focused on you as a reader. Whenever we have a conference, I'll start by asking you how it's been going and what you've been thinking about or working on as a reader. You can tell me what's hard and what's easy. You can tell me what you love and what you hate about reading. You can tell me what makes you want to keep reading and what makes you want to stop. It'll be great if you tell me about the tricky stuff, because then I can try to help.

"In the conference we'll celebrate your progress, look for solutions to the tough stuff, and set some goals together. And since we'll have a conference every week or so, you can always be thinking about things we should talk about next time."

During a reading conference, your attention and your thinking are showered solely on one child. You don't respond to the phone or another student tapping on your shoulder or two students in the corner who appear to be off task. You've worked hard to help everyone understand this is a sacred time and you will purposefully ignore all distractions and interruptions. The only exceptions are true emergencies.

This can be hard at first, because you're going to have to turn off some of your teacher powers, like your *eyes-in-the-back-of-your-head power* or your *try-to-do-four-things-at-once power*. Instead, you'll develop your *intense-concentration-on-just-this-one-thing power* and your *being-in-this-moment-with-this-kid power*.

When you direct this incredible focus toward one student at a time, amazing things start to happen. Even though you might have a whole class of students, what matters is how you reach and teach each one of them individually.

9.1 Recognize and Commit to the Power of One-to-One Conferences

During the conference, you enter the child's reading world, observe what is happening, ask thoughtful questions, listen, celebrate, and coach him on a next step. Conferences are a safe and supportive means for a student to talk about important topics related to her experiences as a reader. Although it starts as a simple conversation, the reading conference has the potential to be so much more.

The Power of Reading Conferences

Reasons Conferences Are So Powerful	Strategic Actions You Might Take
You'll build a stronger relationship with every child in your classroom.	Use your words and actions to put students at ease. Give your complete and undivided attention for a few precious minutes. Paraphrase to ensure the student feels heard and understood.
You'll support the development of purposeful conversation skills.	Patiently listen and give him time to talk. Raise the level of her conversations, through modeling and well-crafted questions.
You'll reinforce high expectations for rigorous reading.	Express confidence that he is capable of wise reading. Ask thought-provoking open-ended questions. Follow up on strategies and procedures you've previously taught. Help the student set and achieve meaningful goals.
You'll engage in meaningful, ongoing informal assessment of every reader.	Think deeply about just this child's choices, progress, and comprehension. Observe his reading skills, successes, and struggles up close.
You'll provide highly differentiated instruction to every child.	Focus on the explicit needs of this student. Identify students with similar needs for small-group work. Identify common needs for whole-group instruction. Customize feedback and support for students at either end of the proficiency scale.

Differentiation

Students these days have more diverse needs than ever before. Some are working to learn English while learning to read. Some have special cognitive or behavioral needs. Some are reading above grade level. Some are reading significantly below grade level. A conference is a perfect way to differentiate your instruction.

Conferring is not *one more thing*. Conferring with your students regularly results in better small-group and whole-group instruction and more interaction with your students throughout the day. In *One to One: The Art of Conferring with Young Writers*, Calkins, Hartman, and White refer to the student conference as "a power chip that will vitalize your teaching forever":

Conferring can give us the force that makes our minilessons and curriculum development and assessment and everything else more powerful. It gives us an endless resource of teaching wisdom, an endless source of accountability, a system of checks and balances. And it gives us laughter and human connection—and the understanding of our children that gives spirit to our teaching. (2005, 6)

Learning to confer well takes time and practice, but it is time well spent. Without this incredible "power chip," your students cannot realize the full benefit of independent reading in your classroom.

9.2 Set an Inviting and Respectful Tone

Many students have very little experience with focused one-to-one conversations with their teacher. Some associate this type of interaction only with being pulled aside because of bad behavior or a struggle to learn. Students new to conferences may become deer in the headlights: *What is this? What's happening?*

Before you hold your first reading conference, let students know what to expect. This will lower their anxiety and empower them to participate at higher levels. Kids, like adults, love getting the inside scoop. You might present a minilesson in which you demonstrate a conference with one of your more confident students or show a video clip of a conference in action.

A conference is a conversation, not a test, an interrogation, or a place to make kids prove they are reading. Five simple but strategic actions will help you establish a sense of caring and equality:

1. **Go to the student rather than have her come to you.** This is an essential way to help a student feel more comfortable. Calling a student up to your desk or teaching table interrupts her reading and often creates a feeling of anxiety.

2. **Get side by side at the student's level.** If the student is sitting on the floor, it's easy to sit down next to him. If the student is sitting at a table or a desk, you can bring a chair or small stool with you or kneel down next to him. Don't stand or lean over the student during a conference; doing so sends a definite nonverbal message that you are in charge and he is subordinate—not the tone you're going for.

3. **Ask permission to interrupt.** If you truly value reading engagement, you need to be gentle and respectful anytime you interrupt a student's independent reading. Consider yourself a guest in the child's reading space and ask permission to interrupt rather than take over from a place of power: "Hey, Martin, can we take a moment to talk about how things are going?" Don't worry. He isn't going to turn you down.

4. **Smile and make eye contact.** Smiling assures the student that this will be a positive interaction. Eye contact signals connection and focus. Without your having to say a word, these two simple actions together let the child know you're happy to be there and she has your attention.

5. **Speak softly.** You don't need or want the whole room to hear you. But you do want the child to be able to hear you clearly and you want to hear her easily too. Use a low, quiet voice, usually just above a whisper. Some teachers call this a *one-foot voice*, intended for people within one foot of the speaker.

> **Reflect**
>
> A teacher is sitting down to visit with a child you love. How would you like that to feel?

9.3 Follow a Predictable Format

You've pulled up a chair, positioned yourself next to the child at eye level, and been welcomed by him into his reading space. Now comes the part you may fear most of all. How do you know what to say? Will you know what to teach? What if he doesn't say anything interesting or meaningful? What if you don't know how to respond?

There is no right or wrong thing to say in a conference; follow the student's lead. However, you want to avoid unfocused and meandering conversation. Lucy Calkins and the staff at the Teachers College Reading and Writing Project have dedicated enormous time and energy over several decades to studying and refining the process of conferring with students. Calkins suggests a consistent pattern of steps for effective conferences: *research, decide, teach*, and *link*. Following this predictable structure will help you keep your conferences efficient and meaningful. The stages are summarized in the following sections.

Four Stages of a Conference

Phase 1: Research

In the first few minutes of the conference, you are a researcher, studying the student. Your job is to ask, observe, and listen—to gather information with two goals in mind:

* Identify a meaningful *compliment* you can give the reader.
* Discover a powerful *teaching point*.

Although you will sometimes have an idea of what you want to compliment or teach, much of the research should take place within the conference.

> **Keys to the Research Phase of a Conference**
>
> Ask open-ended questions.
> Use wait time strategically.
> Paraphrase.
> Do more listening than talking.

Use lots of nonverbal cues.

Review artifacts.

Give a meaningful compliment.

Ask Open-Ended Questions

Your goal is to ask questions that will get the child to talk about the deep thinking she is doing and the strategies she is using as a reader. Asking open-ended questions is essential to starting and expanding the conversation. Examples include the following:

- How's it going? (Carl Anderson)
- Catch me up. (Peter Johnston)
- How did you choose this book? Tell me about it.
- What have you been noticing so far as a reader?
- What are you discovering about the characters [or topic]?

At first you may want to carry a cheat sheet of basic conferring questions (see Appendix C, available online at www.heinemann.com/products/E06155.aspx) to refer to if you get stuck, the conversation lags, your brain freezes, or the child says absolutely nothing.

Use Wait Time Strategically

After you ask a question, don't be afraid to sit through some silence. Many students have learned that if they don't respond quickly, you will move on or change your expectations. Others aren't able to organize their thoughts in the short wait time you typically provide. Allowing some silence shifts the balance of talk from you to the student. If the silence feels awkward, say, "You're wise to take your time and really think about this. I'll wait." This is a nice reminder to both you and the student.

Paraphrase

Paraphrase briefly what the student says. This lets him know you're listening and that you're trying to understand exactly what he is saying. You might begin like this:

- So you're saying …
- So you're noticing …
- Let me see if I've got this right.

Do More Listening than Talking

Listening more than talking can be hard. You may feel you're not earning your salary if you aren't in charge of the dialogue. But learning to talk less and listen more is the key to getting information you need in the research phase of the conference. "Being a good listener means we have to 'shut up and listen' or how else will we know what we need to teach" (Allen 2009, 127).

Use Plenty of Nonverbal Cues

There are lots of ways to communicate without taking over the conversation. Smile. Nod your head. Let your face show excitement, amazement, or worry as you listen to a description or a retelling. Chuckle, sigh, or gasp if appropriate. Be natural, but make sure the student knows you are both interested and affected by what she is telling you.

Review Artifacts

Consider the reading-related artifacts the student is using to support independent reading, such as reading logs, reading response notebooks, and sticky notes or other forms of annotation. All of these can inform both your compliment and your teaching point.

Give a Meaningful Compliment

Explicitly naming something you see the child doing well is an important way to build both rapport and reader confidence. Tell him clearly what powerful and important thing you've noticed him doing already and make sure he understands that he should continue this same smart thing in the future:

* I notice you're working hard to choose books related to your interests.
* I see that you're noticing tricky words and drawing on all you know to try to solve them.
* You're noticing a lot about the characters, about how they respond to events in the story.
* You're really pushing yourself to try this new and sometimes tricky genre of science fiction.

As the student discovers that the questions you ask result in sincere compliments of his actions as a reader, anxiety will go down and the likelihood of him repeating the identified actions will go up. So, before you jump into teaching, give a clear, meaningful compliment.

Phase 2: Decide

After a few minutes spent gathering focused information and sharing a worthy compliment, switch from your detective hat to your teaching hat. You'll arrive at the decision phase with your mind full of possibilities. Choose just *one* thing to teach this student today. Rely on your research, both what you've learned about this student today and what you've already discovered in the past.

If you've got lots of ideas, how do you quickly select just one? And how do you know it is a good one? Here are some considerations:

* What will help this child become more independent? Any teaching point that will help him carry on more independently and with more confidence is worthy.

* What have I already taught that this student needs me to teach again? If she isn't able to apply previous teaching, reteach something from a previous conference, a whole-group minilesson, a read-aloud, or small-group instruction.

* What will matter a great deal right now? When you have several possibilities for what to teach, choose the one you think will give the biggest bang for the buck.

* What is this child ready for next? Some things he needs are still too far out of reach. Choose something that is a true next step, not a giant leap.

* What will be useful in other texts on other days? You want your teaching point to apply not just today in *this* text but tomorrow and the next day in whatever text the child picks up. Think generalization.

* What will help the child get where *she* wants to go? Teaching is always strengthened when it follows a child's lead. Don't overlook an opportunity to follow her strong cue about where she wants to go.

IF YOU DON'T KNOW WHAT TO TEACH

Sometimes the problem isn't that you have too many ideas but that despite your best attempts at research, you don't know what to teach. Don't panic. There are a number of ways to proceed:

* Consider how well the child is applying what you've already taught. Whether it's choosing books, inferring, solving words, or reading fluently, the ultimate goal of your teaching is for the student to apply it to independent reading. If you notice a child having trouble applying strategies that have been previously taught (to the whole group, to a small group, or in a conference), a conference is the perfect time to provide more differentiation.

* Ask the child to read aloud. If conversation doesn't help you clarify a teaching point, listening to the child read aloud often will. You can have him read aloud a favorite part, the last few paragraphs he has read, or the next few paragraphs or pages. This will trigger either a compliment or a teaching point.

* End with a compliment. If you're stuck for a teaching point, give a strong, sincere compliment and move to the next conference. This is fine, as long as you don't fall into the habit of only giving compliments, especially to your most competent readers—everyone needs individualized instruction.

* Ask the student. If you don't identify a strong teaching point yourself, ask the student what she thinks might be helpful or what goals she might set as a reader:

  * What goal do you think you could set for yourself as a reader this week?
  * What do you think you need the most help with as a reader right now?
  * What's still feeling tricky?

If you're frequently stumped about what to teach next in a reading conference, you may want to learn more about the reading process in general and the strategic actions of proficient readers. Check out the resources in Appendix C (available online at www.heinemann.com /products/E06155.aspx) for ideas about great starting points.

Phase 3: Teach

Remember to keep it simple. Once again, the idea is *one* clear teaching point in three or four minutes at the most. This is not a full-blown lesson; it's a bite-size piece of targeted differentiation that will scaffold a reader's ability to use a reading strategy.

Start by clearly naming what you are going to teach, and then teach it, using the same strategies you use in your other teaching. Sometimes you'll show a student explicitly how to do something. Sometimes you'll explain it. Sometimes you'll guide or coach while the child does it. Sometimes you'll use an example or an analogy to make a concept clearer. You're a teacher. You've got this. This is what you do!

Phase 4: Link

The goal of this phase is to connect and transfer the learning from today's conference to the student's future reading habits. A minilesson ends the same way. Essentially, you're telling your student, "This is the important thing we worked on today. You'll want to use this whenever you are reading to help you . . . For example:

* Reading the punctuation as well as the words will make your reading easier to understand. Whenever you're reading, pay attention to what the punctuation is telling you.
* Selecting your books carefully will help you stay engaged as a reader. Whenever you're choosing a text, be sure you find a book you really want to read.
* Reading the words around an unknown word can give you clues about the word's meaning. When you're unsure what a word means, reread the words around it.
* Thinking about what the writer means but isn't coming right out and saying is an important way readers help themselves understand a text. You'll want to keep doing that in this book and in all the books you read.

To help a student remember the teaching point, you could write it on a sticky note or bookmark and ask him to reread it frequently as a reminder of the strategy (see Figure 9.1, for example). Or have the student copy the note onto a page in his reading journal devoted to teaching points made or goals identified in reading conferences. Figure 9.2 provides a simple guide to the four conference phases.

Figure 9.1 Teacher's Sticky Note from a Conference

Figure 9.2 Simple Guide to Four Phases of a Conference

Phase	Goal	What to Remember	Examples
Research	Learn more about the reader through observation and open-ended questions. Provide a focused compliment that he can apply in his future reading.	Listen more than you talk. Choose a compliment that can be generalized.	"How's it going? How did you choose this book? What has been most challenging? What strategies have you found useful?" "I notice that you are working hard to stay focused on the book about sharks, even though it is challenging. Reading things we care about makes us want to keep reading and work hard."
Decide	Decide what one thing you will teach this student today and how you will teach it.	Select just one teaching point. What matters the most right now? What learning is just within his grasp without being too difficult? What is he focused on? What have you been working on in past minilessons, small groups, or conferences?	The child has chosen a challenging book about a topic he loves. He has not read nonfiction books at this level before and is focusing on the main text more than the features. You could help him make the text more manageable by making sure he understands the power of gleaning all he can from the text features before digging into the narrative.
Teach	Teach the student through demonstration and guided practice or by explaining and showing an example.	Keep your teaching clear and concise.	"Watch what I do when I go to a new page of text in this book about sharks. Before I read the paragraphs, I spend time studying the illustrations, reading the captions, and thinking about the information there. This helps me learn some important information before I start reading the main text. "Let's try this out together on the next page. Which features might give you some background knowledge before you start reading the main text?"
Link	Connect and transfer the learning to the everyday life of the reader.	Specifically name the teaching point one more time and remind him to use it in the future.	"When you're reading nonfiction, remember there is important information tucked into lots of text features on the pages. Taking time to study the features will help you better understand the text."

9.4 Create a Conferring Routine That Works

Making conferences a regular part of independent reading takes time and practice. The more conferences you conduct, the more comfortable you'll become. Give yourself permission to be a beginner and work your way through the nitty-gritty details and questions that often come up in the early days. The following sections may help.

How Much Time Should I Spend with Each Child?

Keep it short and focused, especially in the beginning. You want more than a surface check-in, but there are three reasons to keep it short:

* If you spend too much time in each conference, you'll feel overwhelmed.
* Your students are trading valuable reading minutes to confer with you. Keeping it short shows that you respect the importance of getting back to reading.
* It helps you avoid the urge to overteach and instead focus on one important compliment and one important teaching point.

How long is short? In the beginning, while you're training yourself and your students on what to expect, you'll want to keep your conferences to five minutes at most. As you build confidence and get to know your readers, you may occasionally go longer.

How Much Conferring Should I Tackle in a Day?

Although some experienced teachers mix conferring and working with small groups within the same independent reading session, if you're new to conferring, you'll find it cleaner to designate certain days as conference days and others as small-group days. On conference days you can focus all your energy on effective conferences; you'll improve with each repetition. If you spend twenty to thirty minutes conferring with students for four or five minutes each, you'll easily meet with five or six students a day, and your whole class in a five-day cycle.

How Do I Decide Which Students to Meet with Each Day?

To make sure you meet with all students regularly, create a schedule (see Figure 9.3). Determine how many days it will take to confer with every student in the class (using numbers rather than days of the week allows you to accommodate vacations or schedule changes). Start each day with the students most in need of a conference. Their conferences will most likely take longer, and doing them first ensures they don't get skipped. You can adjust the rest of your time if they do run long.

Help! I Can't Get to Everyone!

If you struggle to get through a complete cycle of conferences within a reasonable time or have trouble sticking to your schedule, here are some suggestions:

Figure 9.3 Sample Conference Plan for the Week

Weekly Conference Planning Sheet

Week of ___9/9 - 9/13___

Monday 9/9	Tuesday 9/10	Wednesday 9/11	Thursday 9/12	Friday 9/13
Kristopher	Justin	Crystal	Aaron	Emma
Katrina	Nora	Miranda	Devin	Maria
Nadia	Miguel	Kimi	Delia	~~Lorenzo~~ absent
adam	Beau	josie	alicia	Kashwanda
Soren	Cory	mak	Leah	

Week of ___9/16 - 9/20___

Monday 9/16	Tuesday 9/17	Wednesday 9/18	Thursday 9/19	Friday 9/20
Kristopher	Justin	Crystal	absent ~~Aaron~~ ↦ Emma	
Katrina	Nora	Miranda	Devin	Maria
Nadia	absent ~~Miguel~~ ↤ Kimi		Soren	Leah
adam	Beau	josie	~~Delia~~	Kashwanda
~~Lorenzo~~ ↤ Cory		mak	~~alicia~~	

Week of ___9/23 - 9/27___

Monday 9/23	Tuesday 9/24	Wednesday 9/25	Thursday 9/26	Friday 9/27
Soren	Lorenzo	Cory	Delia	Emma
Kristopher	Justin	Miranda	Devin	Maria
Nadia	Nora	Absent ~~Crystal~~ ↦ aaron		Cory
~~adam~~	~~Miguel~~	Kimi	alicia	Kashwanda
~~Katrina~~	~~Beau~~	josie	~~Leah~~	

✱ **Pay attention to length.** Make a point of checking the start and end time of your conferences (a stopwatch app on your phone also works well). You may be surprised to find you are spending ten or twelve minutes instead of four or five. Pushing yourself to stick to shorter conferences in the beginning will help you develop a natural rhythm over time.

✱ **Shorten the parts.** The research and decide phases of the conference are typically only a couple of minutes, and the link should take less than a minute. Most of the time is spent teaching. If your conferences are running long, evaluate which parts need to be tightened.

✻ **Try some small-group conferences.** When you are working on procedures and routines, when certain students have common needs, or when your day gets shortened for any reason, consider inviting a small group of students to participate in a conference together.

✻ **Focus on compliment conferences.** Focusing on the research and compliment phases helps you learn the qualities of a good compliment and manage a class of children who may be new to independent reading (Serravallo and Goldberg 2007). Starting off with a few rounds of shorter compliment conferences for everyone in the class

  ✻ allows you to practice the research and compliment phases
  ✻ helps your students view conferences in a positive light
  ✻ ensures you get around to everyone several times in quick succession.

Compliment conferences are also an important tool anytime things fall apart during independent reading; they are an efficient way to remind students what high-quality reading looks like and reinforce the behavior and strategies you want them to exemplify.

Conference Tip

Don't compliment something superficial or old. Look for something the student is doing that is new or emerging, that was previously a struggle, and that really matters.

How Do I Take Notes During the Conference?

Keeping notes during a conference can be tricky. Even people who've been conferring for a while struggle to find their note-taking groove. Taking notes for the sake of taking notes is a waste of time and effort. However, a well-designed note system helps you

  ✻ keep track of the important things you notice a reader doing
  ✻ plan for what a reader might need in the future
  ✻ monitor progress
  ✻ identify common strengths and needs in the class.

I've observed dozens of teachers try dozens of systems over the years, from note cards to mailing labels to electronic tablets. Ultimately, the simpler the system, the more likely you will be able to maintain and benefit from it. If it's too cumbersome or complicated, you won't find the energy to keep it up. This one is super simple:

1. **Get a clipboard.**

2. **Prepare a class schedule** (see Figure 9.3) of whom you plan to confer with each day (see also Appendix C, available online at www.heinemann.com/products/E06155.aspx).

3. **Prepare a conference record sheet,** a class roster with names down the left-hand side and some boxes after each child's name. Each time you meet with a student, add the date to the right of her or his name, thus easily keeping track of whom you have and have

not recently conferred with. Tape this sheet to the back of the clipboard, or keep it in the front of your conferring notebook, so you can access it at all times (see Figure 9.4 and Appendix C).

Figure 9.4 Sample Conference Record Sheet

Conference Record Sheet

Student Name	Conference Date								
Kristopher	9/9	9/16	9/23						
Justin	9/10	9/17	9/24						
Miranda	9/11	9/18	9/25						
Delia	9/12	9/26							
Lorenzo	9/18	9/24							
Katrina	9/9	9/16							
Miguel	9/10	9/18							
Crystal	9/11	9/18	9/26						
Aaron	9/12	9/20	9/25						
Josie	9/11	9/18	9/25						
Nadia	9/9	9/16	9/23						
Adam	9/9	9/16							
Nora	9/10	9/17	9/24						
Emma	9/13	9/19	9/27						
Maria	9/13	9/20	9/27						
Devin	9/12	9/19	9/26						
Kimi	9/11	9/17	9/25						
Kashuanda	9/13	9/20	9/27						
Beau	9/10	9/17							

4. **Prepare a separate note-taking sheet for each child.** Place these sheets on your clipboard in the order you'll meet with your students, with day one students on the top, followed by day two, and so on. Appendix E (available online at www.heinemann.com /products/E06155.aspx) includes a simple two-column grid for recording strengths and compliments as well as needs and teaching points. Draw a line under both columns to separate the notes from each successive conference and indicate the date.

5. **Take notes.** During each conference, the page for that child will be the top one on the clipboard, where you can write on it. After the conference, move it to the bottom, exposing the next child's page. (Be sure to record the date of each conference on the conference record sheet taped to the back of the clipboard.)

6. **Move the completed note-taking sheets to a tabbed binder.** As the sheets of notes fill up, place them, along with any other reading artifacts, in a binder with a tabbed section for each student (see Figure 9.5). You now have a comprehensive record of the individual observations and differentiated instruction you've provided to each child over time.

Figure 9.5 Photo of Conferring Notebook

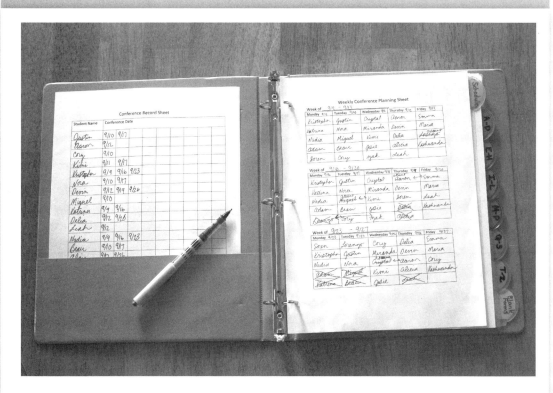

Modify the system so it works for you. The important thing is that it is manageable enough that you can maintain it and meaningful enough that you use your notes to guide your instruction. That's the only worthwhile reason to take notes in the first place. Figure 9.6 lists some ways conference notes can help you. Once you get started, you're going to fall in love with them!

Figure 9.6 What Should I Do with the Information I Gather?

Conference notes can help you . . .	For example . . .
Better understand what makes a student tick or shuts him down.	Ronald seems to need lots of wait time to formulate his thoughts. I want to remember this in group situations.
Formulate small-group instruction for kids with common needs.	Several students are reading longer books now and need to understand the importance of looking back at the beginning of a reading session to pick up the thread from the day before.
Think about what books you might recommend to a child.	Heather has been reading the same chapter book series about horses for several weeks but hasn't read any nonfiction this year. Maybe I could encourage more variety by sharing some nonfiction about horses.
Inform your choices for your classroom library.	Lots of boys have fallen in love with Matt Christopher books recently. We could use more of them in our library.
Notice things about which the whole class would benefit from more instruction.	When I ask students to share a favorite part, it takes so much time. I want to teach them all a system for using sticky notes to highlight favorite parts.
Rediscover all the things that can be tricky for readers.	I'd forgotten how hard it can be to keep track of all the characters in a novel, especially when the names are unfamiliar. I need to think of a good strategy to help students with this.
Identify areas about which you need more information in order to meet your students' needs.	Terry continues to choose books that are way too difficult, and I've exhausted every strategy I know that might help him. I need help. I'll ask a colleague to brainstorm with me.
Engage in personal reflection about what works and doesn't work.	I'm trying to use open-ended questions, but I still don't feel I'm getting my kids to do much talking in conferences. What can I do to remedy this?
Find points of success and celebration.	Every student I visited with today was able to state clearly why she or he had chosen the book she or he was reading. It's time to celebrate making informed book choices!

Reflect on Chapter 9

The best advice I can give you about conferring is to trust yourself. Conferring is the backbone of successful independent reading. But it can be tricky business and is only learned with practice. This book is about digging in and getting started. So, summon your courage and allow room for a little uncertainty and imperfection. Think about this chapter's starting points. Which of them are you already doing? Which are you getting ready to implement? (See Figure 9.7.)

Figure 9.7 Steps to Get You Started with Conferring Today

Starting Point	What You Can Do Starting Today
Recognize and commit to the power of one-to-one conferences.	Consider the list of potential conference benefits. Identify a few that are especially important to you and make a visible representation of these reasons to help you stay committed: ✱ Post a sticky note on your computer: "Conferences matter because . . ." ✱ Make a sign: "I'm committed to conferences because . . ." ✱ Have someone take a picture of you in a conference and attach a caption: "I confer because my kids need . . ."
Set an inviting and respectful tone.	Help yourself feel more comfortable during a conference by considering ways to build success in the beginning: ✱ Review the five ways to set the right tone. ✱ Print out a list of example questions; review them frequently or carry the list with you. ✱ Start small. Try it today. Experience how amazing it can be!
Follow a predictable format.	✱ Learn the four phase procedure for a conference; research, compliment, decide, teach. ✱ Reflect at the end of each day, and recognize your successes. ✱ Read more or ask for help when you struggle or get stuck.
Make conferring a regular part of your routine.	Make concrete preparations that will help you stick to a regular schedule of conferring with your students: ✱ Tell your kids you're going to start conferring. ✱ Ask a trusted friend or colleague to check in periodically and ask you how it's going. ✱ Commit to twenty-one consecutive days of conferring. It's a great way to establish a long-term habit. ✱ Make adjustments along the way, but don't give up!

Now reflect on how you'll celebrate success and overcome obstacles as you incorporate conferences into independent reading in your classroom. (See Figure 9.8.)

Figure 9.8 Chapter 9 Reflection and Planning

Reflect on the Process

As I work to establish a conferring practice, I'll recognize success and celebrate along the way by . . .

Something I think might be especially challenging is . . .

The personal strengths I can draw on when I struggle are . . .

Outside resources I can draw on when I'm unsure are . . .

TEN

TALK ABOUT READING

Support, Share, and Expand the Love of Reading Through Conversation

> Students tend to learn more deeply and in more lasting ways when they do the following: repeat and reword their ideas; explain their ideas to a partner; compare their ideas with those of another; support their ideas with examples and experiences from their lives; create new ideas with a partner; listen and have to respond; have their ideas challenged; challenge another's idea; have to figure out new words used by a partner.
>
> —Jeff Zweirs and Marie Crawford, *Academic Conversations: Classroom Talk That Fosters Critical Thinking and Content Understandings*

Bring your classroom alive with engaging, student-driven conversation about reading:

1. Fine tune your teacher language to support deeper thinking and conversation (pages 120–123).

2. Teach students the basics of academic talk by making turn-and-talk a classroom staple (pages 123–129).

3. Routinely have response partners, or reading buddies, converse about books and reading (pages 130–136).

In the real world, people read and then they talk. My husband reads the newspaper and pauses to comment on an article, read a snippet aloud, or ask my opinion about something. Later at dinner with friends, someone asks, "Did you see that piece in last night's paper about...?" and we all

Get Your Students on Board

"One of the greatest things about reading is that it gives you so many ideas to talk about with one another. Talking with others about our reading lives makes reading more important and more meaningful. As we read, we often find things we want to talk about later, and so we tuck them away in our pockets like little gems. We keep them with us until we have a partner to share them with. Then, together we'll turn them over and over through conversation, and, if we're lucky, we'll sometimes discover new colors and markings, things we hadn't noticed before. Reading is great on its own. But when we read and then talk about our reading with a partner, it can be even better. This year, we'll have lots of chances to talk with one another, sharing the great things we are reading, seeing our ideas in different ways, and discovering things we hadn't noticed on our own."

share our ideas and opinions. I read a book I love, and I can't wait to recommend it to the people in my life who I think will love it too. A friend and I who have both read the same great novel make a special date to compare perspectives, dissect the characters, and relive the best parts. A colleague reads about an instructional innovation and forwards the information for me to read and respond to.

Just as you can't wait for kids to be fluid readers before you give them books, you can't wait for them to be experienced conversationalists before you let them talk! Student-led conversation, scary and messy as it can sometimes feel, is probably the most authentic extension of independent reading. Learning to talk about what you read in meaningful ways is a skill required in the college classroom, in the workplace, and in life's many social situations. If you are looking for authentic work to pursue in the reading classroom, you've found it.

Bringing more talk into your classroom doesn't cost a penny. It doesn't create any additional paperwork to lug home and correct. Talk is fun. It's easy. It's good for language development. It deepens learning. And it helps strengthen classroom relationships. So, what are you waiting for? Let your students start talking!

10.1 Fine-tune Your Teacher Language to Support Deeper Thinking and Conversation

To encourage high-quality, academic student conversation, examine your own communication choices throughout the day. Subtle shifts in the words you use can have a powerful effect on student thinking and talk.

Use an Invitational Tone

An invitational tone means using both words and actions that show you know your students have interesting and important ideas to share and you want to hear them. Choosing words that show students you *want* to hear their thinking is a simple adjustment (Johnston 2004):

* I'm *curious to hear* what you are thinking about this character's actions.
* I'm *eager to hear* what clues you've noticed the author giving us.
* I'm so puzzled by this. It will be *interesting to hear* your ideas about what might be going on.

Listen Intently

Too often we listen to students halfheartedly or while sharing their attention with another task or person. In this way-too-busy world, valuing our students' thinking enough to listen with our full attention—wanting to understand what they have to say—is one of the most important gifts we can give them. "The critical conversational act is listening carefully and genuinely. Nothing you can say is more important than this" (Johnston, Ivy, Faulkner 2011, 235).

Practice Revoicing Student Thinking

Revoicing (Ferris 2014; O'Connor and Michaels 1993) is restating what a student has said, asking whether you have understood correctly, getting clarification if necessary, and then holding the thinking up for further consideration by others:

* So, you're saying . . . Is that right?
* Let me see if I heard this right. You're thinking . . . Is that right?
* I hear you disagreeing with the idea that . . . Is that right?
* Let's all take a moment to consider what Anthony just said. . . .

Use Open-Ended Prompts

Open-ended prompts encourage a deeper level of thinking rather than probe for the "right answer." The conversational prompt you choose plays a monumental role in determining the quality of the thinking and conversation that follow. Figure 10.1 lists questions that invite and encourage many ideas and perspectives.

Provide Enough Wait Time

Biting your tongue and providing the golden silence called *processing time* can be as important as the questions you pose. The power of a great question is lost if it's not followed by enough wait time. When you provide those few precious seconds between question and response, the quality of the conversation that follows increases dramatically. Wasik and Hindman (2013) suggest that in many cases up to ten seconds may be needed.

Figure 10.1 Conversational Prompts to Encourage Diverse Ideas and Perspectives

Purpose	Possible Open-Ended Prompt
To explore why	What do you *imagine* are some reasons . . . ?
To explore how	What do you *think* are *some ways* . . . ?
To encourage visualization	Talk about the *things* you are *picturing*. . . .
To extend learning	What are *some examples* you can *think* of that . . . ?
To review past learning	What are *some things* you *remember* about . . . ?
To activate prior knowledge	What are *some ideas* you already *understand* about . . . ?
To make connections	What *connections* are you making as you *think* about . . . ?
To predict	What *predictions* are you making?
To notice	What are you *noticing*?

Support Effort and Growth

Another powerful language shift is to focus feedback on process and effort rather than solely on the end product. Dweck (2006) calls this a shift from a fixed mindset to a growth mindset. A growth mindset reflects a commitment to keep growing and changing through effort and openness to new ideas. Simple shifts in language like those in Figure 10.2 nudge students to think about their own thinking (metacognition) and help them identify strategies that will support their future success.

Make Read-Alouds Interactive

There is no better place to practice this cluster of teacher language skills than during an interactive read-aloud. You make read-alouds interactive by making purposeful language decisions:

* Where will you stop for a turn-and-talk?
* What high-quality open-ended questions will you pose?
* What academic language structures will you encourage by the sentences you frame?

Figure 10.2 Teacher Language to Encourage a Growth Mindset (Dweck 2008)

Comments That Simply Praise the End Result	Comments That Encourage Reflection on Effort and the Use of Strategies
Great job. You did it.	Wow. You really worked hard to figure that out. Tell me about what you did.
Good. You found a book that you like.	I noticed that you took some extra time to make your book selection. What sort of things did you consider?
Good. You got it.	How did you do that?
That's right. You read a tricky word.	How did you figure out that tricky word?
That's right.	What strategies did you use to help you?
Do you need help?	How will you go about finding a solution?

Model Thinking Aloud

The think-aloud is your primary tool for showing kids what is going on inside your reader's brain. Because thinking aloud is a learned skill, you will get better at it only by practicing. To begin, insert the word *thinking* into your instructional language:

- ✖ As I read this part, I am thinking to myself . . .
- ✖ So I'm thinking . . .
- ✖ Listen as I share my thinking about how to tackle this. . . .
- ✖ Now I am thinking to myself . . .
- ✖ At first I was thinking . . . , but now I am thinking maybe . . .

 ## Make Turn-and-Talk a Classroom Staple

Although there are many strategies for bringing more authentic talk into your classroom, a simple and powerful way to begin is the turn-and-talk, in which the entire class participates in focused partner conversation at the same time. You pose a worthwhile question or topic, and two students who are sitting side by side face each other and exchange ideas (see Figures 10.3 and 10.4). You listen in on the thinking being expressed and bring the group back together after a few minutes. Benefits of turn-and-talk include:

✱ Everyone, not just a few eager students, participates.

✱ Students develop oral language skills.

✱ Everyone has the chance to share his or her thinking in the time it would typically take to call on two or three students.

✱ Moving around the room, you can informally assess the thinking of many students in just a few minutes.

✱ Students who are hesitant to speak up have a low-pressure setting in which to verbalize their thinking.

✱ Knowing that everyone will be held accountable for sharing her or his thinking helps students stay tuned in.

✱ Ideas are often repeated, giving students many chances to absorb new learning.

✱ It can be used in every content area.

✱ It prepares students for more complex interactions such as cooperative learning groups, book-clubs, and literature circles.

✱ It moves students toward Common Core standards.

✱ It equips students for respectful and engaged conversations anywhere with anyone.

Figure 10.3 Difference Between Traditional Classroom Conversation and Turn-and-Talk

Figure 10.4 Jobs During Turn-and-Talk Anchor Chart

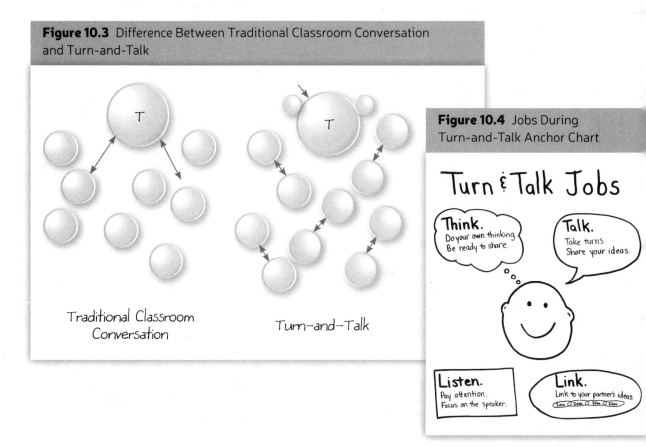

Five Ways to Promote Strong Academic Conversations

Following are five things you can do to promote strong academic conversations in your classroom. None of the five can be introduced once and checked off the list; they all require ongoing effort. But every one of them is an entry point you can choose today, even with your youngest learners.

1. BUILD A CLIMATE OF RESPECT

When building conversational skills, nothing matters more than instilling an expectation of respectful interaction at all times. This includes listening carefully, sharing the floor, and valuing diverse opinions. If students believe there is a chance their ideas will be laughed at or disregarded, they will be much less likely to share openly, take risks, or expand their thinking.

Potential Teaching Points Related to Respectful Conversation

* I look at my partner.
* I listen carefully to what my partner says.
* I take turns with my partner.
* I respect my partner's ideas even if I don't agree.
* I show interest and try to learn more when my partner's ideas are different from mine.
* I use a clear but low voice so that everyone in the room is better able to focus.

2. TEACH STUDENTS TO STAY FOCUSED ON THE TOPIC

Students don't just need more chances to talk; they need to talk in meaningful ways, focused on content.

Potential Teaching Points Related to Staying on Topic

* I take time to do my own thinking before I talk.
* I keep my own conversation focused on the topic.
* If we start to talk about other things, I respectfully say, "We're off topic."
* I ask, "What else?" if we are having a hard time keeping our conversation going.

3. TEACH STUDENTS TO CONNECT THEIR IDEAS TO THE IDEAS OF OTHERS

To prevent a conversation from becoming a disconnected jumble of individual ideas, students need to learn meaningful ways to connect their contributions to the ideas of the other people in the conversation.

Potential Teaching Points Related to Connecting Ideas

* I listen carefully for points of agreement, disagreement, and confusion.
* I practice connecting my thinking to my partner's thinking.
* If I agree or disagree, I explain why.
* If I don't understand what my partner is saying, I ask for more information.
* When my partner doesn't understand my ideas, I offer clarifying examples, analogies, or information.

4. Teach Students to Provide Text-Based Evidence

Students (and teachers) help one another engage in deeper thinking by asking for evidence and proof of the claims being made in conversations. Learning to stretch one's thinking and back up claims with evidence is a foundational theme of the Common Core standards, and even the youngest readers can do this.

Potential Teaching Points Related to Using Text-Based Evidence in Conversation

* I connect my ideas back to evidence from the text.
* I find a place in the text that supports my ideas.
* I look for more than one example of an idea.
* I ask my partner for evidence to support ideas.
* I think about the evidence my partner cites, finding it in the text.

5. Teach Students to Expect Their Thinking to Change

Changed thinking is a sign of learning. Conversation, especially when parties disagree, is a great opportunity to learn more about a person or topic. Teaching students to expect their ideas to change over time is a great way to support a growth mindset (Dweck 2006).

Potential Teaching Points to Encourage a Growth Mindset

* I can learn from my partner.
* I know partner conversations are more interesting when we each have our own ideas.
* I am interested in my partner's ideas, even when they are different from mine.
* I am looking for ways to make my thinking stronger.
* I expect my ideas to change over time.

Ways to Ensure Successful Turn-and-Talks at Any Age

It can be scary to let your kids have more opportunity to talk—at any grade level. But the suggestions below will help ensure success for you and your students from the beginning.

TEACH EXPECTATIONS GRADUALLY AND EXPLICITLY

Don't rush. Like anything worth teaching, helping students acquire the skills needed for meaningful partner conversations takes time. Anyone can turn kids loose to talk with their partners, but you want to teach the skills required for respectful, connected, meaningful conversations.

* Teach one thing at a time.
* Explain why each component matters.
* Model explicitly, using a student as your partner.
* Provide practice at each step of the way.
* Maintain consistent expectations.

PAIR STUDENTS STRATEGICALLY

Although you'll eventually want students to be able to turn and talk with anyone in the room, pairing students strategically in the beginning increases the chances of success and reduces time lost to hurt feelings and unproductive conversations. Assigning the same partners for a week or two at a time lets students become more comfortable working together and have deeper and more focused conversations.

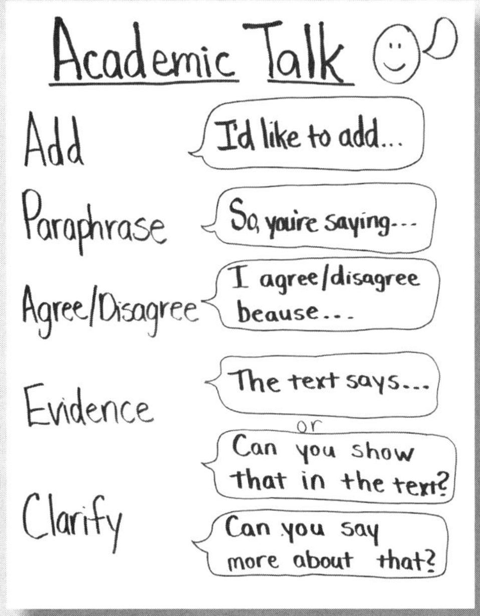

OFFER SENTENCE FRAMES TO HELP STUDENTS CONNECT THEIR IDEAS

Many times students may be talking about the same topic but one person's contributions are still disconnected from his or her partner's. To counteract this, give your students lots of practice with using phrases that help connect conversations, that link one thought to the next. Using sentence frames for connection, like those in Figure 10.5, may feel awkward at first, but doing so pushes students toward deeper listening and thinking.

As you introduce these connectors individually, write them on sentence strips or an anchor chart and place them where they are easily visible. Have all students try them out in a turn-and-talk.

Figure 10.5 Academic Talk Anchor Chart

To connect through agreement or disagreement	I agree and . . . I disagree because . . . I had a similar idea. . . . I had a different idea. . . .
To connect by adding on	I also noticed that . . . One more idea might be . . . What you said about . . . made me wonder . . . What you said about . . . made me remember . . . What you said about . . . made me think about . . .
To connect by getting more information when you don't understand	Can you say more about . . . ? Could you give an example of what you mean by . . . ? Could you clarify what you mean by . . . ?
To connect by telling what changed your thinking	What you said about . . . is making me rethink . . . What you said about . . . is helping me to . . .

WATCH THE TIME

Keep turn-and-talks short, especially in the beginning. Given too much time, kids lose focus and get off track. Listening as students talk provides clues about what you might need to reinforce, introduce, or clarify and helps you know when to pull kids back together. Fight the urge to direct your attention elsewhere. Kids will take their cues from you about how focused and accountable this talk needs to be.

CELEBRATE SUCCESS AS A CLASS

When you are helping your students learn to participate in partner conversations, be sure to recognize what is going well. Give specific compliments to individual students, partnerships, and the class as a whole:

- I noticed Ben and Krista looking right at each other. It was clear they were both focused on the conversation.
- I appreciated the way everyone used a low voice while talking with partners today. That helped us all get more out of the experience.
- I was impressed when I heard Maren connect her ideas to her partner's by using the phrase "I disagree with that because . . .
- I heard Jonah asking for clarification when he didn't understand what his partner was saying. That's an important way to keep the conversation connected.

REFINE THE ROUTINE UNTIL IT RUNS SMOOTHLY

Every student responds to the demands of turn-and-talk in slightly different ways. Be a good observer and reflect on what will make the strategy successful in your classroom. Keep the five ways to promote strong classroom conversations in mind, and keep looking for ways to raise the rigor of these conversations as your students get better at them (see Figure 10.6).

Figure 10.6 Ten Simple Ways to Turn-and-Talk About Independent Reading

Topic	Supporting Sentence Frame
Talk with your partner about the ways you succeeded as an independent reader today.	I succeeded as a reader today by _____.
Talk with your partner about something that has been challenging for you as a reader this week.	Something that has been challenging for me as a reader this week has been _____.
Talk with your partner about the ways you plan to help yourself become a stronger reader in the coming month.	I plan to help myself become a stronger reader by _____.
Talk with your partner about how you solved an unknown word during your reading today.	I solved a difficult word by _____.
Talk with your partner about how a character in the story you are reading has begun to change.	I have noticed that _____ has changed in the following ways: _____.
Talk with your partner about the things you considered when choosing your current book.	When choosing this book, I thought about _____.
Talk with your partner about your plans for reading during the holiday break.	During the holiday break, I plan to read _____.

10.3 Make Partner Conversation About Books and Reading a Daily Routine

Once your students are comfortable with basic turn-and-talk routines, you are ready to begin a new strategy in which response partners, or reading buddies, have conversations about their independent reading. These conversations are fun for students and an authentic means of deepening reading comprehension. They differ from turn-and-talk conversations in three primary ways:

1. They are more student directed.

2. They involve more student choice about both text and topic.

3. They require some student planning.

Turn kids loose with partners to just talk about books? How will you keep them focused? What if they don't know what to talk about? Don't worry, your kids can do it. Really. Even in kindergarten. It will take trust and patience, and you'll need to model what you expect. But once they've gotten the strategy down, you're going to love it. More important, so will your kids! Following are some ways to help your students apply the skills they learned during turn-and-talk to more student-directed conversations with their reading buddies.

Step Inside a Classroom

Partner Conversations with Revoicing

Mrs. Black's third graders, surrounded by book tubs, are scattered throughout the classroom, reading at a variety of levels in any number of genres. Each student has a stack of sticky notes she or he uses to mark points of interest and take notes (an anchor chart reminds them of the types of things they might notice). After about twenty-five minutes, Mrs. Black taps her wind chimes to get the students' attention. "It's time to review your sticky notes and select something that you think would be most important to talk about with your response partner today."

Jonah begins paging back through his book, reviewing the sticky notes. After rereading several, he moves the note about the leopard gecko from the side of the page to the top (a trick Mrs. Black taught to help her students find their talking-point note during the conversation).

"All right, now join your partner. When you are talking today, be sure you practice the new skill of revoicing what you hear your partner say."

---

continues

Jonah meets Mirabelle on the floor next to Mrs. Black's easel, their usual meeting spot. He sits down directly across from her, their knees not quite touching. "How's the reading going today?" he asks, using the respectful and on-topic way to greet a response partner that Mrs. Black has taught the students.

"Really great," Mirabelle replies. "I just started a new book, and I'm already on the third chapter. I didn't want to stop!" She pauses, wanting to share the floor, and asks, "How about you?"

"Pretty good. I spent most of my time studying this book about lizards. I really want to get a gecko or iguana or something for a pet, so I'm trying to learn more about them so I can convince my parents. Can I go first today?" Mirabelle nods in agreement. (Mrs. Black no longer designates which response partner goes first; she's taught students a variety of ways to work this out themselves.) "I chose this note about the spotted gecko being one of the easiest reptile pets to care for." He points to the place on the page and turns it toward Mirabelle.

Mirabelle glances at a list of conversation connectors in her reading notebook and says, "Can you say more about why that is so important to you?"

Jonah nods vigorously. "Because if I tell my parents this is one of the easiest reptiles to take care of, they might think it is a good one for me, since I haven't had a pet before."

Recalling the revoicing technique they've been practicing, Mirabelle says, "So you're saying that because it is an easy pet to take care of, your parents might let you get it. Is that right?"

Jonah nods. "And if I do more research about exactly what to do with a gecko, they'll have to say yes."

Mirabelle nods too. "I agree. I think doing research about it shows responsibility, and parents always want to talk about responsibility, especially with pets."

Make These Conversations Routine, Not an Occasional Event

Regular practice matters. For students to develop the skills needed to have deeper, more engaged conversations, partners must meet regularly. When kids know conversations with their partners will happen in the same way every day (or at least at regular intervals), they become more skilled at both preparation and participation. Carving out five minutes every day will put you on the road to success.

Assign Partners Carefully

Your students probably no longer have formally assigned partners when they turn and talk. However, you should give a great deal of thought to which students you pair as response partners. Some considerations are shared in the list that follows.

Considerations When Pairing Response Partners

* **A student who tends to dominate conversations** might best be paired with another student who is not afraid to speak up. Both partners will benefit from working on the skill of sharing the floor with someone equally talkative.
* **A student who is shy or reluctant to speak up** often benefits from being paired with a student who is patient and willing to share the floor. Sometimes pairing two relatively quiet students also works well; both get lots of practice filling empty space with conversation.
* **It's OK to pair students with varied reading levels** but it helps if the levels are similar. Relative equality within the relationship allows partner conversations to double as book recommendations and makes it easier to share text-based evidence.

Have Response Partners Meet in the Same Location Every Time

Having designated meeting locations lets the transition from independent reading to partner conversation happen quickly and smoothly. The location for each pair should be

* comfortable
* spacious enough for the partners to sit face-to-face and knee-to-knee, either on chairs or on the floor
* far enough away from other partner locations to minimize distractions and allow the partners to hear each other easily
* somewhere easy for you to observe and listen in.

Formally Teach the Skill of Greeting

Greeting each other as readers quickly and informally establishes a climate of interest and respect from the first moment and encourages rich, spontaneous conversations. This greeting can be some form of "So what's happening with your reading today?"

Teach a System for Managing the Conversation

One approach for managing a conversation is to alternate which partner talks first from one meeting to the next. Halfway through the conversation, announce that it's time wrap up talking about the first partner's topic and switch to the second partner's. You can also teach students strategies for deciding who will go first on their own—anything from rock, paper, scissors to asking and offering. Starting off with a more formal system and then leaving it up to the partners as they become more comfortable with the strategy works well.

Explicitly Suggest Things Students Might Talk About

Your students will need explicit suggestions from you about how to shape their time together. Figure 10.7 lists possible topics to engage partners in academic conversation about books and reading.

Figure 10.7 Possible Topics for Response-Partner Conversations

Topic	What It Helps Students Learn
Today, tell your partner how you chose a book you are currently reading. What made you think it would be a good fit?	Readers have strategies they use to help determine whether a book will be a good fit. As they read, they keep thinking about whether the choice was a good one and why.
Prepare to tell your partner why the book you are reading is or is not a good fit for you.	Readers are thoughtful about book choice, trying to recognize what makes some books better fits than others.
Think about a book you would like to recommend to your partner. Why do you want to recommend it?	Readers don't recommend every book they read. They recommend the best books and make recommendations for certain purposes.
When you meet with your partner today, describe the kind of reader you would recommend your book to and why.	Readers think carefully about which people to recommend a book to, knowing that certain books are a better match for certain people.
Select a favorite quotation [paragraph, page, etc.] to read to your partner today.	Readers select certain portions of their books to share with others, letting them in on the greatness of the books.
Think back to the best book you've read this year [week, month, today]. What made this book so much better than the rest?	Readers try to zoom in on the thing that makes one book stand out from others.
When you meet with your partner today, describe the main character in your story in a way that would help your partner prepare to meet him or her.	Readers often want others to meet and know about the characters in a book they are reading.
Today during your conversation with your partner, explain the big challenge that the main character in your story is facing.	Readers describe books to others by including the big challenge.

continues

Figure 10.7 Possible Topics for Response-Partner Conversations, *cont.*

Topic	What It Helps Students Learn
While you're reading today, select a few interesting events in your story that will help your partner understand something about the main character.	Readers think about characters in books and share their observations with others.
Explain to your partner the plan you have for your next trip to the library.	Readers often make plans before they visit the library.
While reading your nonfiction book, mark three important facts to share with your partner. Be ready to explain why you think they are important.	Readers determine which facts are most important when reading nonfiction.

Use Anchor Charts to Help Kids Select Topics Worth Talking About

Deciding what to talk about can be tricky in the beginning, but with practice, support, and patient coaching, it gets easier. When students know they will have a brief partner conversation about their reading every day, they read with a new sense of anticipation. They internalize the kinds of questions that lead to strong conversations. Figure 10.8 lists examples of questions and sentence frames that help students develop a sense of what to talk about with their partners.

Figure 10.8 Getting Ready for a Reading-Buddy Conversation

What I Can Look for to Prepare	How I Might Start the Conversation
What am I enjoying?	I really like the part where . . . because . . .
What is interesting?	I found this part about . . . really interesting because . . .
What is confusing?	I am confused about . . . because . . .
What surprised me?	I was surprised by . . . because . . .
What was funny?	I thought . . . was really funny because . . .
What am I learning?	I am learning . . .
What am I noticing about the characters?	I am noticing . . .
Would I recommend the book? Why or why not?	I would [would not] recommend this book to . . . because . . .
What will I remember about this book?	I'll always remember . . . because . . .

Have Students Prepare for Conversation with Sticky Notes

There are lots of ways students can identify things they might want to talk and think more about with their partners, but marking them with sticky notes is simple and effective. Having younger students use simple symbols (see the anchor chart in Figure 10.9) ensures that marking talking points doesn't take too much valuable time away from reading. Older students need to write only a few key words to remind them what they want to talk more about.

Just before the reading-buddy conversations, each partner reviews her or his sticky notes and selects the one she or he believes is most important to talk about. In the beginning, each partner may talk about a number of sticky notes, because the ideas aren't yet deep or developed. But gradually, we want students to develop the ability to talk longer about a single note (Calkins 2001). Learning to use supportive prompts to stretch and expand each other's thinking helps this along.

Figure 10.9 My Notes Anchor Chart

My Notes
☺ I liked it.
☹ I didn't like it.
! Surprise!
? Question?
☁ I learned.

A kindergarten teacher wonders: "Writing even a few words on a sticky note will take some of my students several minutes, and even then they may not be able to read the notes they've written. Won't this all become a distraction from the primary task of reading?"

A possible solution: The anchor chart in Figure 10.9 shows one way to simplify note taking for kindergartners. They learn these symbols quickly and enjoy adding them to a note. Alternatively, you could give students a set of sticky notes with the symbols already added and have them reuse the notes day after day; students will be able to mark potential talking points more quickly and won't have to manage a pencil.

In addition, the emergent-level books these students are reading typically take only a few minutes to read in their entirety. You could have each partner select and read an entire book to the other student. When they begin reading longer books, they can choose a favorite page to read aloud.

Have Response-Partner Conversations Midway Through the Independent Reading

It works well to have students conduct their conversations halfway through the independent reading time. In kindergarten and first grade, the change of pace and chance to interact with a buddy for a few minutes help stretch stamina and engagement. The same is often true for intermediate students, especially in the fall or when you are first working to build stamina.

Expect Challenges, and Address Them with Ongoing Coaching

There is plenty that can go wrong as we work to build skills for successful reading partners. Choosing conversation topics that fit well is much like choosing books that fit well. Kids fumble around a bit in the beginning. They choose things they find they don't have much to say about after all. Or they attempt to retell an entire story with so much detail that their partners become confused or disengaged. Partners get off topic or forget to connect their thinking to each other's comments in any way at all. Partners disagree or run out of things to say.

However, with regular practice and ongoing coaching, students eventually become more skilled at anticipating what will be fun, interesting, or important to talk over with their partners. In doing so, they have yet another authentic reason for purposeful and engaged reading.

Reflect on Chapter 10

As you move forward, remember this is a process. Rely on the read-aloud, together with open-ended prompts, to strengthen your own skills. Keep listening to kids' conversations with an ear toward what they need next, and provide more direct instruction and modeling whenever they need it. And remember to have fun along the way!

You can use the forms in Figures 10.10 and 10.11 to help you reflect on and strengthen the student conversations in your classroom.

Figure 10.10 Chapter 10 Reflection on Use of Teacher Language

How Well Am I Using Teacher Language to Support Conversation?		
Desired Trait	Yes! I'm confident.	Not yet. I'm ready to start to practice in the following ways.
I use an invitational tone.		
I listen intently.		
I use open-ended conversation prompts.		
I revoice student contributions.		
I provide enough wait time.		
I use teacher language to support effort and growth.		
I use conversation to make read-alouds more interactive.		
I model by thinking aloud.		

Figure 10.11 Chapter 10 Reflection on Actions to Promote Academic Conversation

How Well Am I Promoting Strong, Academic Conversation in My Classroom?	Yes/No	Celebrations/Plans/Comments
I have built a climate of respect.		
Students stay focused on the topic.		
Students connect their ideas to the ideas of others.		
Students provide text-based evidence.		
Students expect their thinking to change.		
Students are able to turn and talk as a class and in small groups.		
Response partners have good conversations about their independent reading.		

ELEVEN

TEACH COMPREHENSION STRATEGIES

If the purpose for reading is anything other than understanding, why read at all?

—Stephanie Harvey and Anne Goudvis, *Strategies That Work:*
Teaching Comprehension to Enhance Understanding

Teach your students to use comprehension strategies during independent reading:

1. Recognize three simple truths about effective strategy instruction (pages 140–142).

2. Identify specific strategies proficient readers use (pages 142–151).

3. Use annotation tools to strengthen comprehension (151–153).

4. Keep strategy instruction in perspective (page 154).

Reading is making meaning of text. Nothing else.

Yes, your students need to learn to decode words; develop their vocabulary, fluency, and stamina; and choose good-fit books. But these skills matter only because they contribute to readers' ability to make meaning of what they read:

* Learning to decode words efficiently allows them to shift their mental energy from figuring out words to figuring out meaning.
* Vocabulary and word work equip them with tools for deriving the meaning of unfamiliar words.
* Building stamina helps them read longer, more complex passages and hold onto their thinking over many pages, chapters, and books.
* Fluency helps them add phrasing and expression to the voices in their heads, making the author's intent clearer.

11.1 Recognize Three Simple Truths About Effective Strategy Instruction

In my early years of teaching, I mistakenly believed that asking lots of comprehension questions, up and down Bloom's taxonomy, meant I was teaching comprehension. I confused comprehension assessment with comprehension instruction. I knew which students had difficulty with comprehension, but I had little idea how to help them. The closest I came was telling students to slow down or read more carefully. My teaching was devoid of any instruction targeted to help students build comprehension strategies. *I* knew how to comprehend, but I was no longer aware enough of my own strategies to recognize them and demonstrate them explicitly to my students. I wish I'd known the three truths about strategy instruction:

1. To teach strategies effectively, you have to observe yourself using them.

2. Strategies are best introduced through explicit modeling and thinking aloud.

3. Conversation and writing are windows into the invisible world of comprehension.

Observe Yourself Using Strategies

I use the windshield wipers on my car all the time. It starts to rain, I put them on. It rains harder, I make them go faster. It stops raining, I turn them off. I get mud splashed on the windshield by a passing car, I put them on and release a few squirts of wiper fluid. I do all of this quite naturally, without thinking about it. If I'm having a conversation or singing along with the radio, I don't miss a beat. I know how to use my wipers both strategically (when it serves a useful purpose) and automatically (without conscious attention).

However, if you were to borrow my car and ask me, "How do the windshield wipers work?" I'd likely struggle to explain. It has become so natural to me and requires so little attention or effort that I'm no longer aware of the steps. Do I twist the handle up or down for faster? Do I push the end of the handle to get fluid, or is the button midway down? The only way to sort this out would be for me to sit in my car, turn the wipers on, watch the process in action, and name the steps in sequence: *Ah, yes, I twist the handle up to get the wipers started, and each additional click up makes them go slightly faster. I push the button on the end for wiper fluid. Touching it once gives a small squirt. Holding it down gives a continuous spray.* After slowing the process down to watch and take note, I would be able to teach you what to do.

The same is true for strategy instruction. As proficient readers, we use many strategies when reading. But they've become so automatic that we have little or no awareness of them. Teaching them is difficult, because we've forgotten what it feels like to use them in a step-by-step way, which, of course, is what we need to do to demonstrate them for our students.

How do you teach something you can't remember clearly how to do? Just as I would have to sit in that driver's seat and observe myself using the windshield wipers, as a proficient reader you need to catch yourself using comprehension strategies, carefully noting the things you do in your own head.

The best way to do this is by reading a text that feels challenging. This might be a newspaper article on a topic about which you have little or no background knowledge, a piece of poetry, or some other genre that you rarely read. When you read something challenging and unfamiliar, you coax your usually underground strategy use into the open. There you can observe and take note of exactly how it helps a reader. Figure 11.1 provides some examples.

Figure 11.1 Examples of Strategy Use in Action

Example	Strategy
I've chosen this book because I'm fascinated by the topic. I'm hoping to find out why.	Asking questions
When reading a technical article, I rely heavily on the section headings as brief introductions to what I'll be reading about. Because they are short and clear, they are a helpful way to prepare my mind for the information that follows.	Determining importance
After reading a tricky paragraph or section, I stop to summarize and then think about how that chunk of information fits with the overall idea of the article.	Determining importance Synthesizing
When I lose my way, I go back a few paragraphs to where I was still understanding to see whether that helps me make an easier transition to the tricky part.	Monitoring and repairing
When a sentence doesn't sound right, I go back to the beginning of that sentence and pay closer attention to each word, to see if I have made a decoding error. As I do this, I think about what would make sense in the sentence.	Monitoring and repairing Activating background knowledge
When I encounter long technical words that I don't know, I look for chunks that I do know. Not only does this help me decode the word more efficiently, but I might find chunks that give me clues about the meaning of the word.	Using schemata Making connections
When I come to a description, I slow down and try to visualize whatever is being described.	Visualizing Creating sensory images
I notice the characters' actions and think about people I know who've acted in similar ways. Then I make inferences about these characters, even though the author hasn't directly stated these things.	Making connections Inferring

Teach Strategies by Modeling Them and Thinking Aloud

Once you've identified a useful reading strategy, make it visible to your students by letting them see it in action:

* **Name and explain the strategy.** Name the strategy and tell students what it is as well as why and how readers use it. "Readers, today I want to show you how asking questions before you start to read can help your mind be alert for certain kinds of useful information."

* **Demonstrate the strategy while thinking aloud.** While reading aloud, pause and explain how you deepen or clarify the thinking "inside your head" (Harvey and Goudvis 2000). "As I prepare to dig into this Seymour Simon book called *Lungs*, I'm wondering what actually happens inside my body as I breathe air in and out and why this whole idea of breathing is so important. As I ask myself these questions, I start to feel even more eager to open the book and start reading. I feel a sense of purpose, because I think reading this book will help me better understand something that I really want to know." The key here is choosing a great text. Modeling deep thinking with a shallow or uninteresting text is like demonstrating diving with a kiddie pool. There are too many great books in the world to teach with anything less.

* **Continue modeling and explaining the strategy over time.** Use a variety of texts and genres, and point out how the strategy works and overlaps with other strategies.

Make Comprehension Visible Through Talking and Writing

Use conversation and writing as windows into the world of thinking. You want using comprehension strategies to become automatic. This requires giving students lots of opportunities to practice. Talking and writing about text while practicing specific strategies deepens comprehension; see Figure 11.2.

Identify Specific Strategies Proficient Readers Use

In recent years much has been written about the specific strategies that proficient readers use (Harvey and Goudvis 2007; Keene and Zimmermann 2007; Miller 2014). To get started, it will be helpful to understand a few basics of the following strategies.

Strategies Proficient Readers Use
. . . .

* Monitoring and repairing meaning
* Making connections
* Determining importance
* Creating sensory images

* Asking questions
* Making inferences
* Synthesizing and summarizing

Figure 11.2 Talking and Writing About Text to Deepen Comprehension

Activity	Benefits	Where to Read More
Talking with a partner during a read-aloud	Read-alouds, in which all students are exposed to rich texts without expending energy on solving words, are great opportunities for students to try strategies. Verbalizing their thinking to partners deepens their understanding.	Chapter 1 Chapter 10
Talking with you in a conference	Conferences are an opportunity to customize strategy practice for the student and the text he or she has selected.	Chapter 9
Participating in small-group instruction	Small groups are the perfect venue for providing additional or adapted practice to students with common needs you've observed in other settings.	Chapter 8
Tracking thinking on sticky notes	This helps students articulate how the strategies they are using affect their thinking (Harvey and Goudvis 2000).	Chapter 10 Chapter 11
Exploring strategy use in a reading notebook	Reading notebook entries provide a glimpse into the thinking students do while reading, evidence of strategies they are using, and clues about other strategies you might teach them (Serravallo).	Chapter 12

Monitoring and Repairing Meaning

Monitoring and Repairing Meaning in a Nutshell

I notice when something isn't right. I slow down and try to fix it.

> In many ways, monitoring is the umbrella under which the other comprehension strategies fall. Each of the strategies is a type of monitoring. When students use them, they automatically revise their thinking as they read. (Keene and Zimmerman 2007, 49)

To monitor and repair meaning, readers need to *pay attention*, noticing when reading is going well and when something doesn't seem right, and *slow down* when they notice a problem and do something about it (see Figure 11.3).

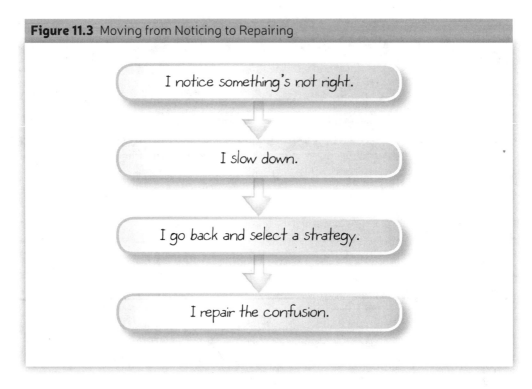

Figure 11.3 Moving from Noticing to Repairing

I notice something's not right.

I slow down.

I go back and select a strategy.

I repair the confusion.

Monitoring is essential to comprehension. Monitoring is training yourself to listen to the voice in your head and notice whether everything is coming together to create meaning or if things are falling apart. It is recognizing when you're thinking, "Huh?" and then figuring out what's confusing or difficult. When you monitor your reading, you ask:

* Did I understand what the text meant, or am I confused?
* Did the text make sense with what I know about the passage? The pictures?
* Did the words I read sound right grammatically?
* Was I engaged in my reading, or did I let my mind wander?

Learning to use fix-up strategies to repair comprehension draws on other aspects of reading skills, such as phonics, language, comprehension, engagement, and fluency. It takes patient teaching over time for students to learn to choose a strategy from an array of possibilities, such as

* going back to reread
* slowing your reading down
* creating a picture in your mind
* thinking about the features like pictures, captions, and headings
* thinking about words that would make sense or sound right
* thinking about what you already know and how that might help you.

Potential Teaching Points Related to Monitoring and Repairing

* Readers know that reading is always about understanding what the text says.
* Readers notice when they are having trouble and try to fix it.
* Readers notice when things don't make sense. They decide what they can do to help themselves understand the text better.
* Readers know that sometimes they have to back up and reread to understand better.
* Readers know that sometimes they have to keep going ahead to get the information they need.
* Readers know that they have to adjust the speed of their reading to their purpose. Some texts need to be read more slowly.

Figure 11.4 Checking My Reading Anchor Chart

Making Connections

Making Connections in a Nutshell

I use the power of what I already know to make learning easier or more meaningful.

Some call it making connections; some call it activating schemata; some call it activating background knowledge. Bottom line: this thinking strategy is using what you've learned or experienced in the past to help you make sense of what you are learning or experiencing right now. Connections help readers make better book choices, stay engaged while reading, and make inferences, and they give readers a foundation on which to attach new learning. The kinds of connections readers make while reading are listed in Figure 11.5.

Figure 11.5 Types of Text Connections Readers Make

Type of Connection	Description	Example
Text to self	The reader makes a connection to a personal experience or piece of background knowledge.	The character is painfully shy and doesn't dare to speak up in class. I am extremely shy and rarely volunteer to speak up in class.
Text to text	The reader makes a connection to another text he or she has read.	In the book I'm reading right now, a group of kids makes fun of another student who is overweight. In the book I read last week, a student was bullied because of the kind of clothes he wore. In both cases, how kids looked on the outside was the cause for bullying.
Text to world	The reader connects with something she or he knows about generally.	We've been studying the election process in social studies. Some of what I've learned there is helping me better understand the book I am reading about a presidential election campaign.

When reading fiction, students make connections with characters, settings, and problems. When the kids in a story have a fight at recess and don't talk to each other for three days, the reader may remember, for example, the pain of an argument she had with a friend the month before and how hard it was to figure out how to overcome the anger and misunderstanding. Both the reader's empathy and curiosity are heightened, and as a result so are engagement and understanding.

Potential Teaching Points Related to Making Connections

* Readers use all that they know to make sense of a text.
* Readers make connections between the text and their own lives.
* Readers make connections between the book they are reading and other books they've read.
* Readers slow down their reading to consider connections.
* Readers often choose books that have a strong connection to their own lives. Connections help them feel more engaged with the text.
* Readers often read a number of texts that are connected in some way (same author, same topic, same series, etc.) in order to expand what they know about that topic.

Step Inside a Classroom

Making Connections Through Read Aloud Conversation

Mrs. D'souza's second graders are gathered on the rug in front of her while she reads Patricia Polacco's *My Rotten Redheaded Older Brother*. In preparation, she has marked with sticky notes places where she will make a connection aloud or have students turn and try the strategy with their partners.

On one page she's placed a sticky note next to the words "The worst was, he was always telling me he could do just about anything better than I." After reading this part, she stops, pauses for a moment, and rereads it. "I'm wondering whether any of you have ever been around someone like that? Think for a minute about what it's like to be around people who think they can do everything better than you." She allows a moment for everyone to do her or his own thinking and then says, "Turn and talk with your partner about any connections you are making with this situation. Use our connections anchor chart if that's helpful." She points to a chart containing sentence frames for starting this kind of conversation.

While the students are talking with their partners, Mrs. D'souza listens in:

MATTHEW: My brother always thinks he can do things better than me. I get so sick of it.

ZANDA: Yeah, my sister is littler than me, and my parents still think everything she does is so great.

BRANDON: I don't have any brothers or sisters, but my cousin thinks he's so much better than me in hockey and basketball and stuff.

BETSY: Last year there was this girl in my class who always thought she was the best at everything we did and it really made me mad because there were lots of kids who were good at stuff, too, and she just thought she was always the best.

Since the rest of the story is about the sister's attempt to find something she can be better at than her brother, this chance to turn and talk is not haphazard but designed to deepen students' understanding of the story and their empathy with the characters.

"It sounds as if many of you are able to make important connections that will help you understand this story better and appreciate what the main character is going through. Let's keep reading."

Determining Importance

Determining Importance in a Nutshell

I identify the most important things I want to remember, the things that matter most.

Not all things an author writes are of equal value. Some are more important than others. To get the most out of what they are reading, readers make decisions about which things are more important to focus on and remember.

In fiction, the most important ideas are usually linked to the theme of the story. Thinking about why the author might have written the story in the first place helps students identify important ideas.

With nonfiction, students need to determine which ideas are big ideas and which are supporting details or simply interesting facts. You can teach students to preview—skim—the text before digging into deeper reading and to pay attention to text features such as boldface, italics, headings, and captions.

Potential Teaching Points Related to Determining Importance

* Readers are always looking for big ideas or themes when they read.
* Readers get clues about the important ideas from the title.
* Headings and chapter titles give hints about important ideas.
* Authors use special fonts (boldface, italics, larger type) to highlight important concepts.
* Readers think about not only the big idea but also how other ideas connect to it.
* Readers look for themes that are true for the characters in the story and for their own lives.

Creating Sensory Images

Creating Sensory Images in a Nutshell

I create images in my mind that deepen my understanding of the text.

Visualizing or creating other sensory images (of how something smells, sounds, feels, or tastes) helps readers make the words on the page come alive. Some teachers refer to this as making pictures or movies in the mind. The images children create in their minds are truly their own, which makes this a great strategy for increased engagement. Students can practice this skill by sketching or describing their mental images. Visualizing is also useful in comparisons (a dog as small as a teacup).

Potential Teaching Points Related to Creating Sensory Images

* Readers paint a picture (or make a movie) in their minds as they are reading.
* Readers read with all their senses (sight, smell, touch, taste, and hearing).
* Creating an image helps readers more fully experience and understand the text.
* Sensory images often help readers make emotional connections to the text.
* Readers change the images in their minds as they encounter new information in the text.

Asking Questions

Asking Questions in a Nutshell

I ask questions to get my brain interested in the text. This motivates me to push forward, searching for information that will help me get clarity and answers.

Asking questions before reading programs your brain to look for certain things as you read. These questions are often the bridge between what you already know about a topic and what you want to learn more about. Then, as you read, you develop new questions. Something in the text triggers a question or makes you wonder about something. *How will this character get out of this situation? Why did he do that? What causes volcanoes? How was television invented?* When these questions aren't answered by the text, the reader may decide to read another text on the same topic to get more information.

Potential Teaching Points Related to Asking Questions

* Readers think about a book before they start reading, using the front and back covers, jacket flaps, and a preliminary skim through the pages to help them wonder about the book.
* Readers come up with questions before, during, and after reading a book.
* Readers revise their questions and come up with new ones as they read.
* Readers sometimes don't find answers to their questions and check another source.
* Readers use questions to read books for special purposes.
* Readers sometimes focus on only those parts of a text that will help answer their questions.

Making Inferences

Making Inferences in a Nutshell

I put what I already know together with information in the text to make a smart guess about something the author has not directly stated.

An inference is an educated assumption you make about something the author implies but does not state directly. You make inferences by bringing your own connections to what the author tells or shows directly. You see a mother in an illustration with a furrowed brow and hands on her hips. You put this image together with what the author does tell you—the son has spent all his money—and infer that the mother is extremely unhappy about this. Your background knowledge helps you infer what a mother might be feeling in a situation like this.

You can help children infer by asking, "What information do you think the author wanted us to fill in for ourselves?"

> **background knowledge + what the text says explicitly = inference**

Potential Teaching Points Related to Making Inferences

- Readers put what they already know together with what they read to form an inference.
- Readers get clues about characters from the way the characters act.
- Readers use inferences to build a deeper understanding of the text.
- Sometimes inferences need to be adjusted later in the text.
- Authors decide which things to tell readers explicitly and which things to let them figure out on their own through clues.
- Readers read on to find out whether what they predicted is correct.

Synthesizing and Summarizing

> **Synthesizing and Summarizing in a Nutshell**
>
> I combine information from my past and from other sources with my learning from this text to create new meaning.

Synthesis and summarization help you keep track of big ideas while you read and fit everything together at the end. You weave together your previous knowledge, the ideas from across the whole text, and even ideas from other texts you have read to reach an overall understanding.

Teaching Points Related to Synthesizing and Summarizing

- Readers retell their stories using a beginning, middle, and end.
- Readers retell the most important parts of their stories to get others interested in the book.

* Readers hold onto ideas from all parts of the book and weave them together.
* Readers weave ideas together from a variety of books and experiences.
* Readers add to or change what they know as they read.

11.3 Use Annotation Tools to Help Strengthen Comprehension

Taking notes—annotating—as we read is another way to slow down, to pay attention. One way to support the comprehension skills developed through close reading, or "reading with pen in hand" (Schmoker 2006) for readers of all ages is by using annotation tools. You already know a lot about annotation. You use highlighters, pens, and sticky notes in your reading all the time—to slow down and pay attention or to mark something in the text to which you want to return. When you annotate, you focus more deeply on something you've decided is important enough to think, talk, or write more about.

Since the introduction of the Common Core State Standards, the concept of close reading has received a great deal of attention. When reading closely, readers decide how to read a text in order to get the most out of it. They may

* slow down
* reread
* notice clues
* make connections
* look for patterns
* jot down notes
* consider choices the author has made.

Some Reasons Readers Use Annotation

To mark something they want to share with another person

To take note of personal responses to a text

To make it easy to find their way back to something they value

To identify questions and things they wonder about

To notice interesting and new words

To jot down favorite quotations precisely

To take note of interesting facts

To mark something that they're confused, puzzled, or surprised about

To identify evidence that supports their questions or theories

To prepare for partner or small-group conversations

Sticky Notes

Sticky notes are the annotation tool of choice in many elementary classrooms, thanks to Stephanie Harvey and Anne Goudvis' landmark book *Strategies That Work: Teaching Comprehension for Understanding and Engagement* (2000, 2007). Although their book is about much more than a sticky note, the sticky note has certainly stuck.

Kids can't mark up the books they read with highlighters or margin notes, and sticky notes are the next best thing. Give each of the students in your classroom his or her own pack of sticky notes for the first time and the kids will likely respond as though they've just won the lottery. Kids love the idea of being able to use these authentic adult tools to leave a trail of their thoughts, wonderings, predictions, and confusions.

Teaching students to use sticky notes in strategic ways takes time and patience. In the beginning, you may want to limit the number of notes students use: "Today, while you are reading, use three sticky notes to mark spots you think you might like to talk more about with your partner." Limiting the number of notes safeguards against their wasteful or overzealous use, supports the skill of determining importance, and ensures that reading remains the primary focus.

Sticky notes come in all manner of colors, shapes, sizes, and brands. But you don't need fancy multicolored ones: the standard light-yellow notes can usually be purchased in bulk at a fraction of the price. The most important consideration is size. Although intermediate students will manage nicely with standard three-inch-square notes, primary students may be more successful with the larger three-by-four-inch rectangles.

Although the notes are small, their potential is great. Figure 11.6 lists some examples, by grade level, of ways you might use sticky notes to help students slow down their thinking by noticing and noting things along the way.

Since annotation highlights something the reader wants to come back to, writing the sticky note is just the beginning. Later, you'll want students to revisit their notes, looking for those that contain thinking they want to explore in conversation or in writing. Following are a few possible prompts to encourage students to revisit sticky notes:

* Select one sticky note you've written that you'd like to think and talk more about in a conversation with a partner.
* Select one sticky note you've written that you'd like to think and write more about in your reading notebook.

In both cases students are identifying an idea they want to say more about. Sticky notes don't tell the whole story; they mark an important place the reader wants to come back to.

Allowing students to leave one or two sticky notes in a book when they've finished it is a way for them to communicate with future readers, reminding them that others have traveled these same pages and interpreted them in their own ways.

Figure 11.6

Grade-Level Examples of Sticky Note Use to Deepen Comprehension

K	Sometimes when you're reading, you might add a sticky note at a place where you make a big connection to something in your own life. You could draw a picture on the sticky note or write some words to help you remember the connection.
1	Sometimes when you're reading, there will be something that you feel you want to talk about, maybe because it's funny, maybe because it's sad, maybe because you are so surprised. This is the perfect time to use a sticky note. Start by drawing a speech bubble, and then write a few words on the note to help you remember why you're so eager to talk about this part.
2	Sometimes when you're reading, you'll have questions. Maybe you'll have questions about what's really going on. Maybe you'll have questions about what's going to happen next or why a character did a certain thing. When you have a question or wonder about something, stop and write a sticky note. This helps you clarify the question and focus your brain on looking for answers or clues.
3	As you notice characters in your story changing in some way, it might be worth jotting your thoughts on a sticky note. Often the ways that characters change give us clues about the author's message. For this kind of note, you could write the character's name and a few words about the changes you've noticed.
4	Readers sometimes have big feelings. When you notice yourself having a big feeling as you read, you may want to mark the place with a word or two on a sticky note. Sometimes we don't understand why we respond to texts so deeply, but it may be important to come back to these big-feeling parts and explore them in our conversations with others and in our writing.
5	Sticky notes are a simple way to remember important facts you may later want to include in your research paper. As you're reading and you notice a fact that directly relates to the question or topic you're researching, jot it down in your own words and write the name of the book and the page number on the note as well. This makes it easy to include and cite the fact later on.

11.4 Keep Strategy Instruction in Perspective

Although strategies are powerful tools for readers, it's easy to lose sight of the forest for the trees when it comes to their instruction. There are three important ideas to help keep a healthy perspective about strategy instruction.

It's Not the Strategies; It's How They Help You Understand the Text

You can get so carried away with having students name and apply strategies that the strategies actually get in the way of comprehension rather than enhance it. Your goal is not to memorize and teach specific strategies but to find meaningful ways to help students deepen their comprehension.

There Is No Particular Order for Teaching the Strategies

One strategy is not more or less difficult than another, and any student at any age or stage of reading development can use all of them. There's not a first-grade set, a second-grade set, and so on. Even nonreaders can use these strategies. What varies is the complexity of the texts in which readers at various levels apply the strategies and the ways in which they combine them.

Using Strategies on Demand Is Unnatural

Although you will teach one strategy at a time, don't insist that students overuse it or use it in unnatural ways. The goal is for students to use all the strategies in natural and overlapping ways while reading independently. Cumulative instruction is important: one strategy is often connected to or leads to another. Proficient readers don't use just one strategy at a time:

* They use past experiences, or *connections*, to generate *questions* about a topic. As they get new information, they *synthesize* it with what they already know.
* Through *monitoring*, they notice that they're confused about a topic. They go back and reread more slowly, trying to *visualize* what the author is describing.
* They make a *connection* to something in their past and create a *mental image* of it, including sights, sounds, and smells, to deepen their involvement in the story.

Enhanced understanding is what matters. "Remember, the strategies are tools. They are a means to an end—comprehension—not an end in themselves" (Keene and Zimmerman 2007, 43).

Reflect on Chapter 11

Use the form in Figure 11.7 to review and reflect on the three simple truths about comprehension instruction.

Figure 11.7 Chapter 11 Reflection on Comprehension Instruction

My Reflections on the Three Simple Truths About Comprehension Instruction

Simple Truth	Possible Action	Reflection
To teach strategies effectively, you have to observe yourself using them.	Locate a nonfiction article on a technical or scientific topic you know little about. As you attempt to understand the article, note the specific strategies you use to help yourself.	
Strategies are best introduced through explicit modeling and thinking aloud.	Plan specific points in your next read-aloud at which you will stop to demonstrate a strategy by thinking aloud. ("As I read this part, I was thinking . . .")	
Conversation and writing are windows into the invisible world of comprehension.	Push yourself to provide more opportunities for your students to talk and write about what they're reading. (Use some of the response prompts in Appendix D, available online at www .heinemann.com/products/E06155 .aspx.)	

TWELVE

Inform Your Teaching Through Daily Assessment

Most educationally significant assessment takes place in classrooms, moment to
moment, among teachers and students.

—Peter Johnston, *Knowing Literacy: Constructive Literacy Assessment*

Use practical and informal assessment tools to make strong instructional decisions:

1. Recognize that formative assessment is the key to smart instructional decisions (pages
156–157).

2. Adopt "What next?" thinking: identify strengths and next steps (pages 157–158).

3. Harvest formative assessment data from tools you're already using (pages 159–163).

4. Try new assessment tools (pages 164–168).

Perhaps you wanted to skip this chapter because the word *assessment* makes you cringe. You may
be so tangled up in standardized assessments that you've lost sight of the power of simpler day-
to-day assessments like observation, conversation, checklists, and running records. But assessment doesn't have to be painful, complicated, or disconnected from teaching. I promise.

12.1 Recognize That Formative Assessment Is the Key to Smart Instructional Decisions

Great reading teachers depend on practical, formative assessments, not just standardized test
scores or reading levels, as tools for getting to know their students as readers with likes, dislikes,
passions, struggles, strengths, and goals. Decision making *is* the art of the teaching profession, and

formative assessment is the key to making strong decisions. It helps you decide what your kids can do already, what they are ready to do next, and how you will help them take that next step.

This chapter describes several formative assessments you can use to guide your instructional decisions, but it's impossible to do justice to such an essential topic in a few short pages. Even more than the suggestions in other chapters in this book, consider the ideas here baby steps. Once you're firmly on your feet, you'll want to dig deeper—learn more, in any way you can, about formative assessment in the reading classroom.

Carl Anderson (2005) uses the term *assessment stance* to describe a teacher's ability to view children as a rich source of information about themselves in the classroom. When you take an assessment stance, you set out to discover what Vygotsky (1978) calls the zone of proximal development, where students are most ripe for learning. To find this zone, you come to work every day alert for evidence that will help you answer three questions:

- What can my readers already do?
- What new learning is within reach for them?
- How can I best support them in acquiring this new learning?

You're already familiar with this theory. You wouldn't introduce preschoolers to baking by having them measure the ingredients or take the hot pan out of the oven. Instead, you'd select tasks more easily within their reach: dumping, stirring, and scooping. When teaching a child to ride a bike, you wouldn't expect her to steer, pedal, and balance all at once. You'd start with simpler tasks and add new skills gradually as you see success and readiness.

The same is true of your readers. You don't expect them to come in the first day, find great books, read for extended periods, have purposeful conversations with their classmates, write deeply reflective entries in their notebooks, and exclaim their love of reading at the end of the day. Instead, you find out what they *can do now* and use that to help you decide what you might *teach in the future*.

The information you need to take an assessment stance in your classroom is already there. You just need a few simple and practical tools to help you make sense of it.

STARTING POINT 12.2 Adopt "What Next?" Thinking: Identify Strengths and Next Steps

Everyone has a unique system for taking notes, but keeping a running T-chart (Anderson 2005) for each child in your classroom will help you organize your notes so you can quickly translate them into instructional next steps. All you need is a blank piece of paper and a pen. Jot the child's name at the top. Draw a line down the center to make two columns. In one column write clues about a student's current skills and strengths; in the other identify possible future teaching points. As you add to it each day, it becomes a running log of the student's growth over time. Date each note if you like, and cross off the teaching points after you've made them or use an arrow to indicate that a next step has become a current skill. (See the example in Figure 12.1.)

Strengths Column	Next Steps Teaching Points Column
What can the child do successfully? ✖ Understand the concepts of print ✖ Work with words ✖ Comprehend what he reads ✖ Read fluently What are his strengths? ✖ Knows and uses strategies ✖ Persistent What do you notice about him that can be of help to you down the road? ✖ Interests ✖ Learning styles	What can the child handle next? What is most beneficial for him to learn next? [Don't take big leaps; think in small, manageable next steps.] What could make learning less of a struggle for him? What would make him more independent?

Gather these T-charts on a clipboard or in a notebook and keep them with you during conferences, small-group work, and whole-class instruction. When a piece of useful information presents itself, jot it down. (If you are caught without the T-chart, jot the information on a sticky note and add it to the T-chart later.)

Figure 12.1 Example of an Individual T-Chart

Two-Column Chart for Observation

Name	Kendra	Level D-E-F
Date	Strengths / Celebrations	Possible Next Steps / Teaching Points
10/2	Choosing high interest books / familiar read alouds	Finding more "good-fit" books by trying out a page.
10/9	uses visual info. to solve words.	attend more to pictures to help w/ meaning
10/17	Book selection ☺ Finding lots of good-fit books (fiction)	
10/23	Enjoying knowing characters in series.	Reading dialogue w/ expression
11/6	Excited to point out key scenes/illustrations in stories	Support w/ retelling using B/M/E
11/13	Slows down and works hard at decoding tricky words.	Teach to "crash" into a word so she maintains meaning. (Say 1st sound right away.)

Harvest Formative Assessment Data from Tools You're Already Using

Once you are familiar with T-charts, you will be able to use them to collect the rich data you mine from other formative assessment sources: conversations, observations, conferences, interest inventories, and reading logs.

Conversations

Pay attention when students talk to you and to one another about their reading. When you set up turn-and-talk or response-partner conversations, listen in. There is so much to be learned by listening:

* What are their passions?
* What strikes them as funny? Sad? Silly? Important?
* What engages and excites them about the books they are reading?
* Do they understand how to have a connected conversation with a classmate?
* What do they know about how to retell or summarize a story?
* What strategies do they know to keep a conversation focused?
* What strategies do they know for getting a conversation back on track if it strays?
* What do they know about how to prepare for a conversation?

Observations

Observation is the most basic assessment tool. Watch the students in front of you as they go about their work as readers and look for evidence of how it's going. Try it today. Grab a clipboard, step back, and watch for a bit. Sharpen and fine-tune your powers of observation. This is your go-to strategy for identifying past teaching that has landed successfully and the things you need to teach next. You'll be amazed at what you discover by watching kids in action as readers:

* Do they start reading promptly?
* Do their reading spots work well for them?
* Are they engaged? What does this engagement look like?
* Are some readers disengaged? What does this disengagement look like?
* What strategies do they know for getting back on track when they lose their way?
* Do they have enough quality books so that they can read for the entire time?
* Do they understand the rituals, routines, and expectations for independent reading? Which ones need to be retaught?
* Do they understand how to use the classroom library?

Conferences

The conference is a great instructional venue that doubles as an assessment gold mine, providing clues about how it's going for a reader, especially when you ask powerful open-ended questions and then listen deeply to what your readers tell you. Information from conferences comes by

* listening to a child read aloud
* having a conversation with a child
* reviewing another assessment tool (reading log, interest inventory, etc.) with a child.

Chapter 9 examines conferences in more depth.

Interest Inventories

Interest inventories (for examples, see Appendix D, available online at www.heinemann.com /products/E06155.aspx) help you find out your readers' reading habits, traits, and interests:

* How does the student see himself as a reader?
* Does the student like to read? If so, what does she like to read?
* Does the child have a strong reading history? Or is reading independently something new?
* Does the child have people and resources in his life to support reading at home?
* What genres, topics, and authors does the reader know about?
* What interests does the reader have (sports, horses, etc.) that she might like to read about?
* Do television shows the student likes reveal a particular interest (mysteries, comedies, sporting events, etc.)?

Interest inventories are often most successful when paired with conversations in which you can fill in the holes and dig a bit deeper.

Reading Logs

Through using reading logs, you'll uncover a wealth of information about reading volume, choices, and habits. A reading log has many purposes, but it's primarily a way for the student and you to think objectively about reading choices, volume, and patterns. Reading logs instill a sense of urgency about logging lots of reading miles. Just as a runner might keep track of the distance she travels during each day's training to document her current efforts and determine future goals, a reader can keep track of books he has read and the time he has spent reading each day.

Readers at different levels need different tools with which to log their reading miles. Appendix D (available online at www.heinemann.com/products/E06155.aspx) suggests a variety of reading logs to get you started with a range of reading ages and stages. Of course you'll have your own ideas for modifying and personalizing these simple starting points. See also the examples in Figures 12.2 through 12.7.

Figure 12.2 Creating a Done Pile

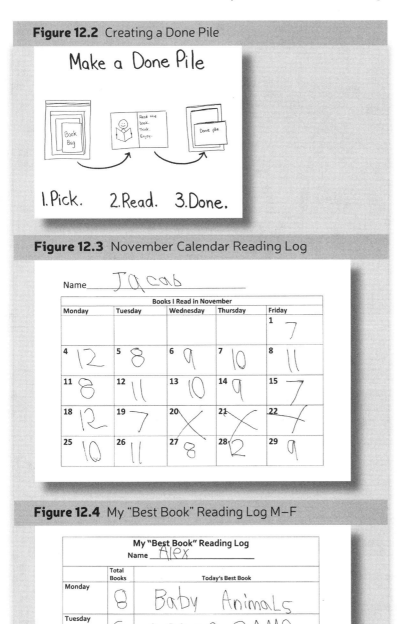

Figure 12.3 November Calendar Reading Log

Figure 12.4 My "Best Book" Reading Log M–F

Figure 12.5 Grades 1–2 Reading Log

Book Log			
Name: John			
Date	Title	Minutes	Pages
3/3	Rise of Balloon Goons	20	1-15
3/4	"	22	16-29
3/5	"	20	30-46
3/6	"	25	47-63
3/7	"	23	64-78
3/10	"	25	79-96
3-11	" Fly Guy "	20	All
3-11	Shark Attack!	24	All
3-12	Rocco Riley Rules	25	1-15
3-13	"	20	16-35
3-14	"	24	36-53
3-17	"	23	54-69
3-18	"	25	70-78

Figure 12.7 Grades 3–5
Reading Log, Part 2 of 2

Book Tracker			
Name: Wendy			
Title: 11 birthdays			
Date	Start/ End Time	Page Numbers	H- Home S- School
1/15	10:10- 10:40	1-24	S
1/15	8:10- 8:25	25-35	H
1/16	10:15- 10:40	36-58	S
1/16	6:00- 6:15	59-70	H
1/17	10:13- 10:43	71-99	S
1/17	5:15- 5:40	100-127	H
1/18	10:10- 10:44	128-165	S
1/19	10:14- 10:38	166-201	S
1/22	10:10- 10:41	202-231	S
1/22	7:10- 7:55	232-272	H

Figure 12.6 Grades 3–5 Reading Log, Part 1 of 2

Reading Log					
(Attach Book Trackers When Complete)					
Name: Wendy					
Date Started	Title	Author	Genre	Total Pages	Date Finished
Sept 8	Confectionally Yours Taking the Cake	Lisa Papademetriou	realistic fiction	240	Sept 16
Sept 17	Confectionally Yours Save Cupcakes	Lisa Papademetriou	realistic fiction	192	Sept 25
Sept 28	Close to Famous	Joan Bauer	realistic fiction	272	Oct 7
Oct 8	My life in pink and green	Lisa Greenwald	realistic fiction	300	Oct 18
Oct 21	My summer of pink and green	Lisa Greenwald	realistic fiction	288	Nov 2
Nov 3	Otherwise known as Sheila the great	Judy Blume	realistic fiction	144	Nov 7
Nov 10	The Candymakers	Wendy Mass	fantasy	480	Nov 27
Nov 30	Betty on the high wire	Lisa Railsback	realistic fiction	288	Dec 6
Dec 7	Harry Potter and the chamber of secrets	J.K. Rowling	fantasy	341	Dec 29
Jan 4	Gilda Joyce Ladies of the Lake	Jennifer Allison	Mystery	352	Jan 12
Jan 15	11 birthdays	Wendy Mass	fiction	272	Jan 22
Jan 23	A crooked kind of perfect	Linda Urban	realistic fiction	224	Feb 3

Whether a simple done pile in kindergarten or a more elaborate record in the intermediate grades, the reading log is a rich source of information about a child's reading choices, preferences, habits, and volume. Figure 12.8 itemizes some of the questions that can be answered by studying a reading log. By regularly studying and reflecting on students' reading logs, you'll uncover amazing patterns and clues relative to your readers that will inform your teaching decisions with regard to individuals, small groups, and the entire class.

Figure 12.8 Questions That Can Be Answered by Studying a Reading Log

Questions That Can Be Answered by Studying a Reading Log	Part of the Reading Log That Provides the Evidence
What type of books is the student reading? Is there variety over time? Does the student appear to have favorite authors? Series? Genres?	Title Genre Author
Is the student finding good-fit books? What level are most of the books?	Time spent with text Title
What about reading volume? How much time is the student spending reading? Is the student finishing books or frequently abandoning them?	Date Number of minutes Number of pages/chapters
What about reading rate? How many pages is the student reading?*	Date Number of pages read per day*
Is the student reading both at home and at school?	Home/school column

*In general, readers of fictional chapter books should read at a rate of about three-quarters of a page per minute silently. Although it may seem strange that a child reading *Cam Jansen* should read at the same rate as a child reading *Maniac Magee*, the truth is that they aren't reading at the same rate. Word-per-minute rate should increase as readers read higher levels, and along with that increased word-per-minute rate, the density of the print on a page becomes greater. In the end it all works out to be about three-quarters page per minute. Reading rate is harder to estimate when reading informational texts since print size, layout, and text features vary greatly within a level. (Serravallo 2014b, 33–34)

Try New Assessment Tools

Now it's time to push yourself a bit, to try out some tools that may be new to you as you work to make wise decisions about what your readers can do and need next. The four assessment tools discussed here—status of the class, roster checklist, reading notebook, and running record—take a little more time to learn, but each offers a powerful way to help you begin to realize the full potential of independent reading in your classroom.

Status of the Class

Status of the class (Atwell) is a simple but powerful record-keeping to help you check in with your readers individually just before, during, or after independent reading each day. First, you decide what you want to know: what book they will be reading, what page they'll be starting on, anything that will help you provide the support they need. Then, using a form you've prepared in advance (see the example in Figure 12.9), you call out each child's name and he or she provides the information and heads for a reading spot. You can also gather the information while you circulate as students are reading or during the sharing session.

Figure 12.9 Example Status of the Class Record

Status of the Class

Name	Date 9/7 Bok/Page	Date 9/10 Book/Page	Date 9/13	Date 9/16
Kristopher	Squish #1 →		Squish #2/ RN	Flat Stanley #4 New
Justin	2030 Start	Magic Tree #14 Start	X	Magic Tree House → 24
Miranda	War 48 →	111	214 →	275
Delia	Just Grace 22	102	RN → 130	X
Lorenzo	3rd Grade Probs 29 →	94	→ RN/New	Horrible Harry NEW
Katrina	Clementine 27 →	90	Pickle Juice Cookie NEW	→ 78
Miguel	Snakes Start	Sharks Start	Spiders New	Rosco Riley #1 Try It. ☺
Crystal	Horses Start	Horses/RN →	Cats vs Dogs NEW	X
Aaron	4th grad Nothing 34 →	101 RN	RN/Encycl Brown NEW	E Brown → 84
Josie	Nat Geo Joking 37	X	X	2 New Need help w/selection
Nadia	Ivy & Bean 14 →	87 →	129	RN New
Adam	Homework Machi Start	56 →	Erupto Start	→ 89
Nora	Clementine 62	Marty McGuire 14	→ 111	RN/New
Emma	Matilda 41 →	194 →	Meanest Doll 98 →	178
Maria	Cam Jansen #4 13	→ RN/New	Cam Jansen #6 New →	48
Devin	Frindle 16 →	78	RN/New	Homework Mach 74
Kimi	Katie Kazo #2 44	Finish/RN	K.K. #3 38	K.K. #4 NEW
Lashwanda	Worst 3r 18	Putter Tabby NEW	Prego NEW	Putter, Tabb NEW
Beau	Harry Potter 32 →	124 →	212	297

You'll still want students to record the same information in their reading logs, but this tool allows you to keep tabs on everyone's progress and plans for the day. Status of the class information is particularly helpful in grades 3–5, when all students are reading longer texts. Figure 12.10 presents two common questions, examples of how students might respond, and why they matter.

Figure 12.10 Example Status of the Class Questions

Question	Student Response	Why It Matters
What will you be doing today?	I'm going to read the whole time. I'm going to start by making an entry in my reading notebook. I'm going to try to read at least six books.	This simple question asked just prior to independent reading each day helps kids mentally plan and commit to how they will spend their time, while simultaneously informing you of their plans, allowing you to easily spot students who may need support.
Where are you in the book you're reading?	I'm going to begin it today. I'm on page 25. Page 215, almost the end.	If you notice students not making much progress or proceeding at an unreasonably fast pace, you might add them to your conferring schedule and investigate.

Roster Checklist

A roster checklist is a simple grid with the names of your students down the side and the skills and strategies you are teaching across the top. As you observe evidence that students have or have not mastered a skill, you mark the grid with a + or a 0. Keeping track of individual learning tells you what skills need more attention, who should get the additional instruction, and whether it will be best delivered to the whole class, in a small group, or individually.

The roster checklist in Figure 12.11 shows five skills a kindergarten teacher taught her class early in the year. She documented on the checklist which skills each student was applying during independent reading and used this information to decide whether to provide more whole-class instruction for a particular skill or whether it would be more effective to work on the skill in a small group or during individual conferences. As you study Figure 12.11 ask yourself:

* Which skills are a good fit for more whole-class instruction?
* Which skills are a good fit for small-group instruction?
* Which skills can best be addressed in individual conferences?
* Which skills don't need any more attention?
* Which students need the most support in mastering these skills?

Figure 12.11 Skills I Taught My Kindergartners in September

Roster Checklist

Name	Go to reading spot and start right away.	Organize space to create a done pile.	Turn pages one at a time.	Read the pictures.	Retell a familiar story.	Point to where to start reading.	Look at partner during turn & talk	Sometimes let partner go first during turn & talk
Desmond	+	→	+	+	—	+	+	+
Jonas	+	+	+	+	+	+	+	+
Hannah	+	+	+	+	+	+	—	—
Isaac	—	—	+	+	+	—	+	+
Sarah	+	+	+	+	+	+	+	+
Riley	—	—	+	+	—	—	+	—
Andrew	—	—	+	+	+	+	+	+
Lizzie	+	+	+	+	+	+	+	+
Aleta	+	+	+	+	+	+	+	+
Ruby	+	—	+	+	—	—	+	+
Joe	+	+	+	+	+	+	+	—
Macy	+	+	+	+	+	+	+	+
Jessi	+	—	+	+	+	+	—	—
Eva	+	+	+	+	+	+	+	+
Maddie	—	—	—	+	+	—	+	—
Ethan	+	+	+	+	+	+	+	+
Molly	+	+	+	+	+	+	+	+
Joe	—	—	—	+	—	—	+	+
Ridge	+	—	+	+	+	+	+	+

Figure 12.12 contains examples of instruction a teacher might provide after reviewing the findings on a roster checklist. Using this process, you'll soon find what Cathy Mere (2005) calls "the right instructional mix" of whole-class minilessons, small-group work, and individual conferences. No instructional format is a silver bullet by itself, but in combination, they pack a powerful punch in your effort to provide learning for all.

Figure 12.12 Using a Roster Checklist for Instructional Planning

Format	Example
Whole-class instruction	Many students are not getting started right away with independent reading. You gather the whole class prior to independent reading, review the expectations anchor chart, and add photos to make these expectations clearer. You use students to model ✳ what getting started right away looks and sounds like ✳ what not getting started right away looks and sounds like ✳ what getting started looks and sounds like one more time.
Small-group instruction	Some students haven't selected enough appropriate reading material to keep them engaged the whole time. You gather this small group during independent reading and remind them of the book-selection strategies you have previously taught to the whole class. You ask students to apply these strategies as they identify books in their boxes that they consider good fits and those that are not. Students exchange their not-so-great choices for new choices in the classroom library and share them with you and the group.
One-to-one conference or partner conference	One student frequently talks to classmates during independent reading. In a one-to-one conference, you help her brainstorm ideas about how to overcome this behavior. Together you decide she needs to try out a different spot during independent reading. You offer two choices and agree to check back with her the next day.

Reading Notebooks

Reading notebooks are a powerful source of information about readers. Writing is thinking made visible. A reading notebook is not only a tool for keeping kids accountable but also a treasure trove of concrete evidence of and information about their thinking as readers:

✳ Are they making personal connections in their reading?
✳ Do they see the connections between texts with similar characters or themes?
✳ Are they making predictions and inferences?
✳ Are they able to summarize and synthesize?

* Do they love the texts they choose?
* Are they asking powerful questions?

Once you're comfortable having your kids talk about their reading and use sticky notes to begin making important annotations, implementing reading notebooks will be a logical next step. I don't expand on it here, because it isn't exactly a simple starting point. But when you're ready, it is an essential way to deepen and expand your readers' thinking, help students write to sources (as required by the Common Core State Standards), and track their growth in making meaning of what they read. When you feel ready, Appendix D (available online at www .heinemann.com/products/E06155.aspx) has some resources to get you started.

Running Record

The ability to take and analyze a running record on any text a child is reading is an indispensable skill that every reading teacher eventually needs to learn—you can't teach reading at the highest levels without this tool. The simplest, clearest resource is a little book written by Marie Clay (the mother of Reading Recovery and running records), *Running Records for Classroom Teachers* (2002). You can also ask your building literacy coach, reading interventionist, or Reading Recovery teacher for information and guidance or consult the free training videos on YouTube.

Running records help you understand many things about a reader:

* Is she reading at the appropriate level?
* What is her instructional reading level? Independent level? Frustration level?
* What is her rate of accurate reading?
* How often does she self-correct errors?
* Does she have a well-developed system for self-monitoring while reading?
* Does she use visual information efficiently? Meaning? Sentence structure?
* Does she read fluently? Frequently omit words? Repeat words?
* Does she frequently appeal for adult help?
* What strategies does she most often use at the point of difficulty?

Reflect on Chapter 12

Students' independent competence is your ultimate goal, no matter what you're teaching—riding a bike, tying shoelaces, making a sandwich, doing long division, selecting books. To take learners from dependence to independence, follow these steps:

1. Figure out where the learners are right now in relation to the ultimate goal (formative assessment).

2. Determine which steps are within the learners' reach (zone of proximal development).

3. Teach the task explicitly, then gently decrease the level of support to help move the learners to a higher level of independence (gradual release of responsibility).

4. Provide differing additional levels of support to some learners based on their response to your teaching (differentiation).

5. Begin the cycle again (ongoing assessment).

Use Figure 12.13 to think about how to make the most of your assessment.

Figure 12.13 Chapter 13 Reflection and Next Steps

Reflect on Possible Next Steps

What sources of ongoing day-to-day formative assessment do I currently rely on in my reading classroom?

How could I use a running T-chart immediately to make more sensible instructional decisions?

Which of the other formative assessment tools in this chapter feel most comfortably within reach for me to start to use immediately?

What goals can I set for myself to make sure I continue to expand my use of formative assessment to support independent reading?

Conclusion

Some Courage for the Journey

> You can, you should, and if you're brave enough to start, you will.
>
> —Stephen King, *On Writing: A Memoir of the Craft*

The starting points I've shared here are simply that—beginnings. They are intended to reassure you that starting can be simple. But I must warn you that they are not quick fixes. There are no quick fixes in education—not here or anywhere else. The instruction your students need in order to become authentically literate will require an ongoing, career-long commitment. It will require that you keep asking yourself, "What next?" Most of all, it will require courage.

Why courage? Because it can be scary to make changes. It can be scary to try new things. It can be scary to move from having kids spend most of the time in your reading classroom generating "products and proof" to having kids spend a whole lot of time doing the authentic work of independent reading.

You'll need courage because in the beginning you're not going to know all of the answers and you're going to move forward anyway. You're not going to have the depth of understanding that you will eventually need and want. You're not going to know exactly how to get all of your kids matched with books that will deeply engage them during reading time. You're not going to know just what the content of your minilessons or conferences should be. You're not going to know exactly how this small flexible grouping stuff should work. And because you're not going to know all of the answers, you're going to substitute courage, in order to keep moving forward while you learn more and sort things out. The Courage Rules are a good companion to take along on the journey.

Courage Rules★

1. Start small. But start.

2. Be good to yourself.

3. Keep a sense of humor.

4. Reflect, learn, and adjust.

5. Be in charge of your own learning.

6. Don't give up when it gets hard.

7. Celebrate along the way.

★Important: Follow these rules only if you want to succeed.

Hopefully, you've already implemented many of the starting points suggested in these pages. If not, it's time to go back to the chapter reflections and choose some concrete steps you can take, starting immediately. Not everything—just a few manageable next steps. Once you've begun, it won't be long before that brave and hungry voice inside you starts asking, "What next?"

That's the time to surround yourself with mentors, colleagues, and friends who will continue to support and inspire you. Read, read, read (the "References" list at the end of this book is full of great possibilities). And most importantly, take time for professional reflection. So much of what you need to know to succeed is already inside of you. It's just waiting for a little affirmation and encouragement.

Your kids are waiting.

It's time to bravely begin.

Off you go.

Works Cited

Allen, Patrick A. 2009. *Conferring: The Keystone of Reader's Workshop*. Portland, ME: Stenhouse.

Allington, Richard L. 2009. *What Really Matters in Response to Intervention: Research-Based Designs*. Boston: Pearson.

———. 2012. *What Really Matters for Struggling Readers: Designing Research-Based Programs*. Boston: Pearson.

Allington, Richard, and Rachel E. Gabriel. 2012. "Every Child, Every Day." *Educational Leadership* 69: 10–15.

Anderson, Carl. 2000. *How's It Going? A Practical Guide to Conferring with Young Writers*. Portsmouth, NH: Heinemann.

———. 2005. *Assessing Writers*. Portsmouth, NH: Heinemann.

Atwell, Nancie. 1998. *In the Middle: New Understandings about Reading, Writing, and Learning*. 2nd ed. Portsmouth, NH: Heinemann.

———. 2007. *The Reading Zone: How to Help Kids Become Skilled, Passionate, Habitual, Critical Readers*. New York: Scholastic.

Boushey, Gail, and Joan Moser. 2012. "Big Ideas Behind Daily 5 and Cafe." *The Reading Teacher* 66 (3): 172–78.

———. 2014. *The Daily 5*. 2nd ed. Portland, ME: Stenhouse.

Burkins, Jan M., and Melody M. Croft. 2010. *Preventing Misguided Reading: New Strategies for Guided Reading Teachers*. Newark, DE: International Reading Association.

Calkins, Lucy. 2001. *The Art of Teaching Reading*. New York: Longman.

Calkins, Lucy, Mary Ehrenworth, and Christopher Lehman. 2012. *Pathways to the Common Core: Accelerating Achievement*. Portsmouth, NH: Heinemann.

Calkins, Lucy, Amanda Hartman, and Zoe White. 2005. *One to One: The Art of Conferring with Young Writers*. Portsmouth, NH: Heinemann.

Clay, Marie M. 2002. *Running Records for Classroom Teachers*. Portsmouth, NH: Heinemann.

Cohen, Robin. 2008. *Developing Essential Literacy Skills: A Continuum of Lessons for K–3*. Newark, DE: International Reading Association.

Collins, Kathy. 2004. *Growing Readers: Units of Study in the Primary Classroom*. Portland, ME: Stenhouse.

———. 2008. *Reading for Real: Teach Students to Read with Power, Intention, and Joy in K–3 Classrooms*. Portland, ME: Stenhouse.

Cunningham, Anne E., and Keith E. Stanovich. 2001. "What Reading Does for the Mind." *Journal of Direct Instruction* 1 (2): 137–49.

Diller, Debbie. 2007. *Making the Most of Small Groups: Differentiation for All*. Portland, ME: Stenhouse.

———. 2008. *Spaces and Places: Designing Classrooms for Literacy*. Portland, ME: Stenhouse.

Dweck, Carol S. 2006. *Mindset: The New Psychology of Success: How We Can Learn to Fulfill Our Potential.* New York: Random House.

Ferris, Sarah J. 2014. "Revoicing: A Tool to Engage All Learners in Academic Conversations." *The Reading Teacher* 67 (5): 353–57.

Fountas, Irene C., and Gay Su Pinnell. 1996. *Guided Reading: Good First Teaching for All Children.* Portsmouth, NH: Heinemann.

———. 2012a. *The Fountas and Pinnell Prompting Guide for Oral Reading and Early Writing.* Portsmouth, NH: Heinemann.

———. 2012b. *The Fountas and Pinnell Prompting Guide Part 2, for Comprehension: Thinking, Talking, and Writing.* Portsmouth: Heinemann.

———. 2012c. *Genre Study: Teaching with Fiction and Nonfiction Books.* Portsmouth, NH: Heinemann.

Frey, Nancy, Douglas Fisher, and Adam Berkin. 2009. *Good Habits, Great Readers: Building the Literacy Community.* Boston: Allyn and Bacon/Pearson.

Gallagher, Kelly. 2009. *Readicide: How Schools Are Killing Reading and What You Can Do About It.* Portland, ME: Stenhouse.

Guthrie, John T., and Nicole M. Humenick. 2004. "Motivating Students to Read: Evidence for Classroom Practices That Increase Reading Motivation and Achievement." In *The Voice of Evidence in Reading Research*, ed. Peggy McCardle and Vinita Chhabra, 329–54. Baltimore: Brookes.

Harvey, Stephanie, and Anne Goudvis. 2007. *Strategies That Work: Teaching Comprehension for Understanding and Engagement.* 2nd ed. Portland, ME: Stenhouse.

Hattie, John. 2012. *Visible Learning for Teachers: Maximizing Impact on Learning.* New York: Routledge.

Hidi, Suzanne and Judith Harackiewicz. 2000. "Motivating the Academically Unmotivated: A Critical Issue for the 21st Century." *Review of Educational Research* 70: 151–79.

Hoyt, Linda. 2009. *Revisit, Reflect, Retell: Time-Tested Strategies for Teaching Reading Comprehension.* Portsmouth, NH: Heinemann.

———. 2011. *Solutions for Reading Comprehension: Strategic Interventions for Striving Students, K–6.* Portsmouth, NH: Heinemann.

Johnson, Pat, and Katie Keier. 2010. *Catching Readers Before They Fall: Supporting Readers Who Struggle, K–4.* Portland, ME: Stenhouse.

Johnston, Peter H. 1997. *Knowing Literacy: Constructive Literacy Assessment.* Portland, ME: Stenhouse.

———. 2004. *Choice Words: How Our Language Affects Children's Learning.* Portland, ME: Stenhouse.

———. 2012. *Opening Minds: Using Language to Change Lives.* Portland, ME: Stenhouse.

Johnston, Peter, Ivey, Gay and Faulkner, Amy. 2011. "Talking in Class: Remembering What Is Important About Classroom Talk." *The Reading Teacher* 65: 232–37.

Keene, Ellin Oliver. 2012. *Talk About Understanding: Rethinking Classroom Talk to Enhance Comprehension.* Portsmouth, NH: Heinemann.

Keene, Ellin Oliver, and Susan Zimmermann. 2007. *Mosaic of Thought: The Power of Comprehension Strategy Instruction*. Portsmouth, NH: Heinemann.

Kelley, Michelle J., and Nicki Clausen-Grace. 2009. "Facilitating Engagement by Differentiating Independent Reading." *The Reading Teacher* 63 (4): 313–18.

King, Stephen. 2000. *On Writing: A Memoir of the Craft*. New York: Scribner.

Krashen, Stephen D. 2004. *The Power of Reading: Insights from the Research*. Westport, CT: Libraries Unlimited.

Layne, Steven L. 2009. *Igniting a Passion for Reading*. Portland, ME: Stenhouse.

Martinelli, Marjorie, and Kristine Mraz. 2012. *Smarter Charts, K–2: Optimizing an Instructional Staple to Create Independent Readers and Writers*. Portsmouth, NH: Heinemann.

Marzano, Robert. 2012. *Classroom Instruction That Works: Research-Based Strategies for Increasing Student Achievement*. Denver: McRel.

Mere, Cathy. 2005. *More than Guided Reading: Finding the Right Instructional Mix, K–3*. Portland, ME: Stenhouse.

Miller, Debbie. 2008. *Teaching with Intention: Defining Beliefs, Aligning Practice, Taking Action, K–5*. Portland, ME: Stenhouse.

———. 2014. *Reading with Meaning: Teaching Comprehension in the Primary Grades*. Portland, ME: Stenhouse.

Miller, Debbie, and Barbara Moss. 2013. *No More Independent Reading Without Support*. Portsmouth, NH: Heinemann.

Miller, Donalyn. 2009. *The Book Whisperer: Awakening the Inner Reader in Every Child*. San Francisco: Jossey-Bass.

———. 2012. "Creating a Classroom Where Readers Flourish." *The Reading Teacher* 66 (2): 88–92.

Miller, Donalyn, and Susan Kelley. 2014. *Reading in the Wild: The Book Whisperer's Keys to Cultivating Lifelong Reading Habits*. San Francisco: Jossey-Bass.

Moss, Barbara, and Terrell A. Young. 2010. *Creating Lifelong Readers Through Independent Reading*. Newark, DE: International Reading Association.

O'Connor, Mary Catherine, and Sarah Michaels. 1993. "Aligning Academic Task and Participation Status Through Revoicing: Analysis of a Classroom Discourse Strategy." *Anthropology and Education Quarterly* 24 (4): 318–35.

Oczkus, Lori. 2004. *Super Six Comprehension Strategies: 35 Lessons and More for Reading Success*. Norwood, MA: Christopher-Gordon.

Paterson, Katherine. 2011. "Back from Ibby." The Horn Book. http://archive.hbook.com/magazine/articles/1999/jan99_paterson.asp.

Pearson, and Gallagher. 1983. "The instruction of reading comprehension." *Contemporary Educational Psychology* 8: 317–344.

Pinnell, Gay Su, and Irene C. Fountas. 2011. *The Continuum of Literacy Learning, Grades PreK–2: A Guide to Teaching*. Portsmouth, NH: Heinemann.

Polacco, Patricia. 1994. *My Rotten Redheaded Older Brother*. New York: Aladdin Paperbacks.

Pressley, Michael. 2003. *Motivating Primary-Grade Students*. New York: Guildford.

Rasinski, Timothy V., and James V. Hoffman. 2003. "Oral Reading in the School Literacy Curriculum." *Reading Research Quarterly* 38: 510–22.

Routman, Regie. 2003. *Reading Essentials: The Specifics You Need to Teach Reading Well.* Portsmouth, NH: Heinemann.

———. 2008. *Teaching Essentials: Expecting the Most and Getting the Best from Every Learner, K–8.* Portsmouth, NH: Heinemann.

Reutzel, Ray D., and Sarah Clark. 2011. "Organizing Literacy Classrooms for Effective Instruction." *The Reading Teacher* 65: 96–109.

Serravallo, Jennifer. 2010. *Teaching Reading in Small Groups: Differentiated Instruction for Building Strategic, Independent Readers.* Portsmouth, NH: Heinemann.

———. 2014a. *The Literacy Teacher's Playbook, Grades K–2: Four Steps for Turning Assessment Data into Goal-Directed Instruction.* Portsmouth, NH: Heinemann.

———. 2014b. *The Literacy Teacher's Playbook, Grades 3–6: Four Steps for Turning Assessment Data into Goal-Directed Instruction.* Portsmouth, NH: Heinemann.

Serravallo, Jennifer, and Gravity Goldberg. 2007. *Conferring with Readers: Supporting Each Student's Growth and Independence.* Portsmouth, NH: Heinemann.

Schmoker, Michael J. 2001. "The Crayola Curriculum." *Education Week* 21(8): 42–44.

———. 2006. *Results Now: How We Can Achieve Unprecedented Improvements in Teaching and Learning.* Alexandria, VA: ASCD.

———. 2011. *Focus: Elevating the Essentials to Radically Improve Student Learning.* Alexandria, VA: ASCD.

Stahl, Steven. 2004. "What Do We Know About Fluency? Findings of the National Reading Panel." In *The Voice of Evidence in Reading Research*, ed. Peggy McCardle and Vinita Chhabra, 329–54. Baltimore: Brookes.

Sulzby, Elizabeth. 1985. "Children's Emergent Reading of Favorite Story Books: A Developmental Study." *Reading Research Quarterly* 20 (4): 458–81.

Szymusiak, Karen, Franki Sibberson, and Lisa Koch. 2008. *Beyond Leveled Books: Supporting Early and Transitional Readers in Grades K–5.* Portland, ME: Stenhouse.

Vygotsky, L.S. 1978. *Mind in Society: The Development of Higher Psychological Processes.* Cambridge, MA: Harvard University Press.

Wasik, Barbara, and Annamarie Hindman. 2013. "Realizing the Promise of Open-Ended Questions." *The Reading Teacher* 67 (4): 302–311.

Zwiers, Jeff, and Marie Crawford. 2011. *Academic Conversations: Classroom Talk That Fosters Critical Thinking and Content Understandings.* Portland, ME: Stenhouse.

DA